AF779292

Nicole Elert, Christopher T. Brooks (eds.)
Expats in Germany – Inbound and Outbound

Expats in Germany – Inbound and Outbound

Questions frequently asked by Foreigners

Edited by
Dr. iur. Nicole Elert, Lawyer (Rechtsanwältin) and Specialist Lawyer (Fachanwältin) for Employment Law, Partner, PricewaterhouseCoopers GmbH Wirtschaftsprüfungsgesellschaft (PwC)
Prof. Dr. phil. Christopher T. Brooks, East Stroudsburg University, Pennsylvania

With contributions by
Inga Mayer, Kim Allison Turner, Ife Ashabo, Anne-Inger Bergerhoff, Christopher T. Brooks, Ulrich Buschermöhle, Jacky Chu, Eduardo Depassier, Nicole Elert, Christine Lam, Erik Muscheites, Gennady Odarich, Juliette Schwarz, Mirela Stoia

DE GRUYTER

Editors:
Lawyer Dr. iur. Nicole Elert, PricewaterhouseCoopers GmbH
Wirtschaftsprüfungsgesellschaft (PwC)
Prof. Dr. phil. Christopher T. Brooks, East Stroudsburg University, Pennsylvania

Authors:
Ife Ashabo, Manager – U.S. Immigration Attorney, ife.ashabo@ca.pwc.com
Anne-Inger Bergerhoff, Senior Consultant, anne-inger.bergerhoff@de.pwc.com
Christopher T. Brooks, Professor, East Stroudsburg University of Pennsylvania, cbrooks@esu.edu
Ulrich Buschermöhle, Director, ulrich.buschermoehle@de.pwc.com
Anir Chatterji, Senior Manager – Solicitor (England and Wales) | U.S. Attorney-at-Law (New York), anir.chatterji@pwclegal.co.ae
Jacky Chu, Partner, jacky.chu@cn.pwc.com
Eduardo Depassier, Senior Associate, eduardo.depassier@lpadv.com.br
Nicole Elert, Partner, nicole.elert@de.pwc.com
Christine Lam, Manager, lam.christine@sg.pwc.com
Inga Mayer, Senior Manager, inga.mayer@de.pwc.com
Erik Muscheites, Manager, erik.muscheites@de.pwc.com
Gennady Odarich, Managing Director, gennady.odarich@ru.pwc.com
Juliette Schwarz, Manager, juliette.schwarz@de.pwc.com
Mirela Stoia, Director, mirela.stoia@ch.pwc.com
Kim Allison Turner, Senior Consultant, kim.allison.turner@de.pwc.com

ISBN 978-3-11-040383-1
e-ISBN (PDF) 978-3-11-040401-2
e-ISBN (EPUB) 978-3-11-040404-3

Library of Congress Cataloging-in-Publication Data
A CIP catalog record for this book has been applied for at the Library of Congress.

Bibliographic information published by the Deutsche Nationalbibliothek
The Deutsche Nationalbibliothek lists this publication in the Deutsche Nationalbibliografie; detailed bibliographic data are available in the Internet at http://dnb.d-nb.de.

© 2017 Walter de Gruyter GmbH, Berlin/Boston
Cover image: Rawpixel Ltd/iStock/thinkstock
Data conversion: jürgen ullrich typosatz, 86720 Nördlingen
Printing and binding: CPI books GmbH, Leck
♾ Printed on acid-free paper
Printed in Germany

www.degruyter.com

Preface

The number of foreigners operating in Germany as business travelers, employees or students and the like is growing; so, too, is the number of questions posed by these individuals and firms' HR, tax and legal departments. Reason: there is no debating that German immigration law and administrative practices are quite challenging. Being unaware of the relevant German immigration processes and regulations can lead one to become ensnared in pitfalls that can lead to delay the start of an assignment or a family reunion. Daily questions with respect to 90-day Schengen allowance, university degrees and there possible equivalencies, salaries, local address requirements, proof of health insurance, common law marriage rules, apostille requirements, and many other related matters do arise. Challenging questions about income tax issues, social security aspects and legal protections German law affords employees are often posed by those wishing to work and live in Germany – or by those residing and working in Germany who wish to be outbounded from Germany elsewhere. The global mobility team of PricewaterhouseCoopers GmbH Wirtschaftsprüfungsgesellschaft (PwC) answers these kinds of question on a daily basis and guides foreign employees and their companies through the immigration process.

With this in view, this handbook will serve to answer in writing as simply as possible the questions most commonly posed by those expats coming to work and live in Germany. The focus of this book is to share those questions foreigners commonly ask and then answer them accordingly. We aimed to phrase the questions in a way that an English speaker would formulate them (Note: American English has been chosen for this book). It is a reference book intended to come from a typical business perspective, as opposed to a purely German legal one. It will work to guide foreigners, companies and, in particular, HR specialists through German immigration law, highlighting and explaining basic terms and procedures that non-Germans working in Germany should be aware of. The questions are constructed with a view to standard immigration procedure. This text also includes separate sections that address questions on other pertinent information, including social security, tax, employment law. Each section begins with a brief overview of the specific topic so as to contextualize its application to inbound and outbound matters.

When relevant laws are mentioned, cited or both. However, as the intent of this work is to not be a typical law book, many of the specific citations and references have been left out, because they will be of little interest to our target audience.

Special thanks is owed to Inga Mayer, Rechtsanwältin, Senior Manager, Head of Visa & Immigration, and Kim Allison Turner, Senior Consultant, Visa & Immigration who have put together their decade plus of day-to-day experience in German immigration to write this book. Without their substantial contributions, diligence, and dedication to this project this book could not have been written.

We also thank our global mobility experts to those questions are kindly asked to be addressed to:

Visa and immigration and employment law:
PwC, Inga Mayer, inga.mayer@de.pwc.com
PwC, Kim Allison Turner, kim.allison.turner@de.pwc.com

Social Security:
PwC, Ulrich Buschermöhle, ulrich.buschermoehle@de.pwc.com
PwC, Juliette Schwarz, juliette.schwarz@de.pwc.com

Income Tax:
PwC, Erik Muscheites, erik.muscheites@de.pwc.com
PwC, Anne-Inger Bergerhoff, anne-inger.bergerhoff@de.pwc.com

Questions and amendments regarding this book overall, its concept or tips are kindly asked to be addressed to:
East Stroudsburg University of Pennsylvania, Prof. Christopher Brooks, Dr. phil., cbrooks@esu.edu
PwC, Rechtsanwältin Dr. Nicole Elert, nicole.elert@de.pwc.com

Düsseldorf/East Stroudsburg, November 2016

Nicole Elert, Christopher T. Brooks

Table of Contents

Part 1
Immigration

Part 2
Employment Law

Part 4
Income Tax

List of Abbreviations

%	percent
€	Euro
§	section
Abs.	Absatz
AEntG	Arbeitnehmer-Entsendegesetz
AG	Aktiengesellschaft
AGB	Allgemeine Geschäftsbedingungen
AGB-Gesetz	Gesetz zur Regelung des Rechts der Allgemeinen Geschäftsbedingungen
AGG	Allgemeines Gleichbehandlungsgesetz
aka	also known as
AsylbLG	Asylbewerberleistungsgesetz
AufenthG	Aufenthaltsgesetz
AÜG	Arbeitnehmerüberlassungsgesetz
BAG	Bundesarbeitsgericht
BetrVG	Betriebsverfassungsgesetz
BGB	Bürgerliches Gesetzbuch
BMAS	Bundesministerium für Arbeit und Soziales
BeschV	Verordnung über die Beschäftigung von Ausländerinnen und Ausländern
BUrlG	Bundesurlaubsgesetz
BZSt	Bundeszentralamt für Steuern
CEO	Chief Executive Officer
CV	curriculum vitae
dbb	Deutscher Beamtenbund
DGB	Deutscher Gewerkschaftsbund
e.g.	for example
EEA	European Economic Area
ELStAM	elektronische Lohnsteuerabzugsmerkmale
etc.	et cetera
EU	European Union
FreizügG/EU	Gesetz über die allgemeine Freizügigkeit von Unionsbürgern
GewO	Gewerbeordnung
GmbH	Gesellschaft mit beschränkter Haftung
HGB	Handelsgesetzbuch
HR	human resources
i.e.	that is
IHK	Industrie und Handelskammer
IT	information technology

KSchG	Kündigungsschutzgesetz
MuSchArbV	Mutterschutzarbeitsplatzverordnung
NachwG	Nachweisgesetz
no.	number
OECD	Organisation for Economic Co-operation and Development
para.	paragraph
SCHUFA	Schutzgemeinschaft für allgemeine Kreditsicherung
SchwarzArbG	Schwarzarbeitsbekämpfungsgesetz
sec.	section
SGB	Sozialgesetzbuch
SGB III	Sozialgesetzbuch III – Arbeitsförderung
SGB IV	Sozialgesetzbuch IV – Gemeinsame Vorschriften für die Sozialversicherung
SGB VII	Sozialgesetzbuch VII – Gesetzliche Unfallversicherung
TzBfG	Teilzeitbefristungsgesetz
VAT	value added tax
ZAV	Zentrale Auslands- und Fachvermittlung

Part 1
Immigration

I. Introduction to German immigration

Germany is one of the founding members of the European Union and is a Schengen Agreement signatory. The 1995 Schengen agreement abolished passport and other border controls for those transiting the common Schengen member states' borders[1]. Among the 34 Organization for Economic Co-Operation and Development (OECD) nations, Germany is currently ranked as the second most popular country for immigration[2]. 1

According to the Central Foreigner's registry (Ausländerzentralregister), in 2015, 1,810,904 foreigners immigrated to Germany. This was an increase of 57.6% compared with the same statistic in 2014. Out of the total incoming foreign population in 2015, 1,125,419 were non-EU nationals and 685,485 were citizens of EU countries (excluding Germans nationals returning to Germany). Of the total non-EU nationals, 3.4% came to Germany for employment purposes.[3] 2

The focus of this book is on those foreigners coming to Germany for business or employment purposes, independent of the planned duration of stay (long-term or short-term), or if the foreign worker is a local hire or intra-company transfer. 3

The bulk of the legal framework for this group of individuals can be found in the Residence Act (Aufenthaltsgesetz), Freedom of Movement Act (Freizügigkeitsgesetz), Ordinance on Residence (Aufenthaltsverordnung), and Employment Regulation (Beschäftigungsverordnung). These laws and provisions are interpreted through the Implementing Regulation on employment of foreigners (Durchführungsanweisungen zur Ausländerbeschäftigung) and the Implementing Regulation on the Employment Regulation (Durchführungsanweisungen Beschäftigungsverordnung), both published by the federal employment office (Bundesagentur für Arbeit). 4

The German regulations are affected by European laws and EU directives are being implemented in German national law (e.g. the EU directive on the EU Blue Card was implemented into German national law). 5

With so many different sources for determining the legal grounds for compliance in Germany, many companies struggle to understand how to relocate their employees in a timely manner. 6

1 Austria, Belgium, Czech Republic, Denmark, Estonia, Finland, France, Germany, Greece, Hungary, Iceland, Italy, Latvia, Liechtenstein, Lithuania, Luxembourg, Malta, Netherlands, Norway, Poland, Portugal, Slovakia, Slovenia, Spain, Sweden, Switzerland.

2 OECD (2015), *International Migration Outlook 2015* (Summary), OECD Publishing, Paris. DOI: http://dx.doi.org/10.1787/767acccl-en.

3 http://www.bamf.de/SharedDocs/Anlagen/DE/Publikationen/Broschueren/wanderungsmonitoring-2015.pdf?__blob=publicationFile.

7 Probably the biggest challenge for many companies is the determination of what is classified as business travel vs. travel requiring a work permit. It is not uncommon for companies to send their employees to Germany on business-trip status when they actually require official permission to work. The fast moving needs of the business often override the necessity to be compliant. The possible consequences of this lack of compliance can be read in our chapter on noncompliance.

8 Another challenging situation is the deployment of foreign employees to perform work activities in more than one EU country at the same time. A common work permit for all EU countries has not yet been introduced in order to solve this problem. The work regulations for each EU country are still different and it may be difficult or unrealistic to try to obtain work permits for each required EU country at the same time.

9 A further challenge that companies face when sending foreign employees to Germany is that, through pressures of the business, there is often a big hurry to get the employee to Germany and working as soon as possible. There usually is not enough lead time ensure keeping in line with immigration compliance. This is especially true for shorter term assignments. Unfortunately, Germany does not have a short term work permit type with shorter processing times. Thus, winning work at a client site in Germany can be challenging if the company is not able to get their resources in order quickly. As it currently stands in Germany, irrespective of whether an employee is coming, for example, for 1 month, 6 months or 3 years, the processing times for most work permit types are the same. There is little flexibility for accommodating work assignments where the employee needs to be in Germany quickly.

10 Another common challenge companies have is the need to send their employees to Germany intermittently but over a longer period (e.g. 1–2 years). This usually means spending a few weeks in Germany and then several weeks back in the home country before returning. This situation can be difficult due to the local residential address requirement in order to obtain a long-term work and residence permit and because German immigration authorities stipulate that an assignee must be spending at least 50% of their work time in Germany in order to qualify for a work permit. Intermittent travelers coming to work in Germany will usually stay in a hotel for the few weeks that they are there, however, this is not always the same hotel and German immigration requires the applicant to register an address at the city registry office and be able to receive mail. In addition, the new registration law has made registration in a hotel more difficult (due to the landlord confirmation requirement) and often mail does not reach the recipient there, which can lead to automatic deregistration by German registration authorities. One way around this issue is to secure a company apartment that travelers can use for the duration of the work requirement so they have a place where they can receive mail even if they are out of country.

11 Generally speaking, Germany's immigration procedure is still decentralized, with over 580 immigration offices throughout the country. The immigration offices

for issuing the residence permit are located in each city and administrative district,[4] and a change of residential address to another jurisdiction means a change of responsible immigration office. This can present special challenges, if, for example, the new immigration office assesses a case differently than the previous authority and request additional documentation or even decide that a different permit type applies (exceptions made by one office might not be made at another).

Another tricky point at the immigration offices is determining which documen- 12
tation needs to be submitted for the residence permit application. Each immigration office not only has its own application form (there is no one common form throughout Germany, not even for each German federal state!) but the documents requested vary by office (and even the officer processing the case!). For these reasons, each case needs to be researched individually.

While it is possible to provide general information on processing times and do- 13
cument requirements, there is still a lot of room left for interpretation by the immigration and employment offices and the outcome can always vary from the initial assessment.

Another unfortunate challenge is the reaction time and communication with the 14
authorities. It can be difficult to reach officers by phone, especially during the consultation hours for the public. Unfortunately, it can be very time consuming to try to reach an immigration office by phone to make inquiries or determine the status of an application. E-mail contact can be successful, but response times tend to be very slow, especially on inquiries not already linked to a current application that is being processed. Immigration offices are sometimes understaffed due to illness and vacation absences. It can therefore happen that an application is left unprocessed while the officer is away. In addition, staffing at government authorities is not as simple as in the free economy. Just because an employee shortage is recognized doesn't mean you can go ahead and hire to fill the gap, as there are more bureaucratic processes for hiring in place.

Despite these challenges, Germany still ranks high in popularity for immigra- 15
tion and the discussion on immigration in Germany falls mainly on three populations:

1. **Recent increase of refugees** Germany was faced with a major challenge in 2015 when the number of refugees increased tremendously within a short space of time. The impact of the increased volume of refugees on the labor market and the efforts required to facilitate their integration cannot yet be predicted. The challenges in accommodating this large volume of newcomers still continues. It can be expected that an influx of immigrants of this extent will eventually have an impact on the general development of German immigration.

4 See: https://www.bamf.de/SiteGlobals/Functions/WebGIS/DE/WebGIS_Auslaenderbehoerde.html.

2. **Guest workers and their descendants** Due to the number of guest workers invited to Germany in the 1950s to help build up the weakened German economy, Germany has now had to turn its focus towards the integration of second and third generation migrants who have not returned to their home countries but not fully integrating into German society. The approach to this matter is to facilitate the integration through offering government-subsidized courses (language, politics and culture) and through making these compulsory to those applying for permanent residency, citizenship or both. The integration of this population is an ongoing topic which will require continual analysis, repeated discussion and modification as time goes on.
3. **Highly skilled migrant workers** Since 2012, Germany has strengthened its focus on acquiring highly skilled migrant workers and has been working on making Germany more attractive to highly qualified individuals. The introduction of the Blue Card (see chapter 3.4.) facilitated this initiative, and in 2014 Germany was the EU country that had issued the most Blue Cards.[5]

16 In the past years Germany has seen an increasing lack of highly qualified individuals. This is partially based on the demographic change. Academic studies have shown that Germany (especially in comparison with the neighboring countries Switzerland and Austria) will be disproportionately impacted by the demographic change. In 2030 the German labor market will have approx. 3.5 Million employees less than today[6].

17 This decrease in available labor forces also includes a growing lack of highly qualified personnel.

18 In order to combat the growing lack of skilled personnel, several changes have taken place to simplify the immigration process for this population. The EU Directive for the Blue Card, which supports highly skilled third country nationals to work in EU countries, was implemented into German immigration law in August 2012. This change in the Residence Act eliminates the requirement to seek approval from the German employment office and accelerates the work and residence permission process in Germany.

19 New German immigration regulations implemented in July 2013 brought further changes in immigration processing and introduced the possibility for certain foreigners with a non-university level professional education to also receive a work permit if the requirements are fulfilled. The most significant of these changes was

5 Federal Office for Migration and Refugees http://www.bamf.de/DE/Infothek/Statistiken/BlaueKarteEU/blaue-karte-eu-node.html.

6 Demografischer Wandel: In Deutschland werden Arbeitskräfte rar an Academic Studies published by PwC in 2016.

the elimination of the involvement of the local immigration office in the entry visa process which reduced processing times.

Additionally, the option to apply for a work permit pre-approval has cut down the visa processing time considerably. Previous to 2013, work permit approval was only sought after the visa was filed abroad and forwarded by diplomatic post to Germany, which was a long and tedious process involving several authorities. To a certain extent, this process still exists but is not recommendable. Submission of a visa application with a work permit pre-approval reduces processing time from circa 6–12 weeks down to circa 4–8 weeks. Furthermore, the role of German embassies and consulates abroad became more important, as they were given deciding power over the immediate issuance of the Blue Card (for detailed information about the Blue Card please see chapter 3.4). 20

Despite the facilitation for highly skilled workers, Germany protects its local labor market. There are restrictions for the immigration of workers without academic qualifications, and some work permit categories still require a review to assess whether or not there are unemployed EU citizens qualified for the position and if wage requirements comparable to those of a German national in the same position apply. 21

With all of the recent changes and implementation of new, advanced regulations, the German immigration process appears to be fairly straightforward. Nevertheless, significant challenges still faced include the fragmented set-up of the authority structure and the broad administrative discretion each local authority is allowed to exercise. In a nutshell: What works in Hamburg does not necessarily work in Munich. 22

Further to this background, the aim of this section on inbound immigration is to provide an overview of the general process, the most common immigration categories, non-compliance and penalties and red flags to watch out for when sending foreign employees to Germany. 23

II. Inbound

1 When working on immigration matters it is important to distinguish between the inbound and outbound population.

2 Whilst the inbound population can be defined as foreign individuals coming to Germany, the outbound population refers mainly to German nationals going abroad. When looking at individuals going from Germany to a foreign country, it is crucial to understand that the immigration requirements depend on various factors which are determined by the destination country. Please see Chapter III – Outbound for a general overview as well as more detailed information about a few common destination countries.

3 Counselling on the inbound population is mainly focused on immigration matters (how and when can one legally enter the country and start working?), social security matters (which mandatory payments have to be made?) as well as income tax matters (what income is taxable in which country?). The inbound population includes not only individuals being temporarily sent to Germany by their home employer abroad but also those individuals who sign a local employment contract with a German company. When residing in Germany for either a short or longer period, these individuals are most likely subject to German law in one way or the other (e.g. tax laws, employment laws, social security laws and immigration laws). Hence, the interpretation and perception of the German legislative body and the government authorities have a direct impact on each foreign individual coming to Germany.

4 The requirements for foreigners travelling to Germany for business and/or work purposes are determined by the nationality of the individual. Generally speaking, nationals are divided up into the following categories:

- EU/EEA Nationals
- Swiss Nationals
- Non-Visa Nationals
- Visa Nationals.

5 **EU/EEA[7] Nationals** have, according to the Freedom of Movement Act (Freizügigkeitsgesetz), which is based on the EU Directive 2004/38/EC, the right of freedom of movement and therefore do not require a work permit, entry visa or residence permit for any travel to or employment in Germany. However, they still need to follow German address registration regulations, as does every resident of Germany.

7 EU: Austria, Belgium, Bulgaria, Croatia, Cyprus, Czech Republic, Denmark, Estonia, Finland, France, Germany, Greece, Hungary, Ireland, Italy, Latvia, Lithuania, Luxembourg, Malta, Netherlands, Poland, Portugal, Romania, Slovakia, Slovenia, Spain, Sweden, United Kingdom.
EEA: All EU countries as well as Iceland, Norway and Liechtenstein.

Based on the freedom of movement agreement between Switzerland and the EU, **Swiss nationals** have similar rights to EU/EEA nationals as they also do not require a work permit. However, individuals have to obtain a residence permit (**Aufenthaltskarte**) for stays over 3 months. 6

Certain nationalities are considered **Non-Visa nationals** and do not require an entry visa issued by a German diplomatic post. Nationals of Andorra, Australia, Canada, Israel, Japan, Monaco, New Zealand, San Marino, South Korea, USA are in this category, one that applies to both business/tourist travel, as well as for employment purposes. 7

All other nationalities are considered **Visa Nationals** and can be divided into two sub-categories. While some Visa Nationals (e.g. China, India, Russia) always require an entry visa regardless of the purpose of travel (i.e. business, tourism, studies, employment, etc.), others (e.g. Mexico, Argentina, Hong Kong, Singapore) are exempted from obtaining an entry visa for business (for details on what is considered a business travel, please see chapter II. 1. Business Travel) or tourist purposes. However, they still require an employment visa. The list of exempt nationals is reviewed on an annual basis[8]. 8

For the inbound population, in the following chapters we will provide an overview on what is considered business travel, what is the general process to enter Germany for each of the groups above, what are the most common work permit types (and their requirements)and when is one eligible for permanent residency. Further, we also cover the topics of degree equivalency, family reunion, legalization/apostille, red flags to watch out for and the penalties and fines for non-compliance. 9

1. Business Travel

German immigration law does not contain a clear definition of permitted activities during a business trip, which is why it is sometimes difficult to determine if certain travel is still allowed on a business visitor status. 10

Generally speaking, on a business visit, one may: 11

- attend trade fairs;
- visit a customer market for a product or to negotiate a contract;
- conduct/attend meetings;
- attend classroom training.

Gainful employment, execution of a project and certain forms of training are not allowed on a business visitor status. It is important to note that the duration of stay 12

8 http://www.auswaertiges-amt.de/DE/EinreiseUndAufenthalt/StaatenlisteVisumpflicht_node.html.

is not decisive, but the nature of the activity determines the correct visa category. Thus, it is recommended that one directly contact the immigration authorities in the Germany city where the business traveler intends to stay and to confirm whether the intended activities are allowed under business traveler status.

13 Business trips are often mistakenly used for employment activities that legally require work authorization. This is considered illegal employment in Germany and can have serious legal consequences for both employer and employee.

14 All visitors, regardless of the purpose being business or tourism, are restricted to a maximum stay in the Schengen area of 90 days within any 180-day period. It is important to note that, when counting the 90 days, all days spent in any Schengen country will be taken into consideration. Half days or even a few hours count as one day.

15 Some nationalities will require a Schengen visa stamped in their passport from a German (or any other Schengen country) mission abroad. Other nationals are able to travel for tourist or business purposes on visa waiver status and are not required to obtain this document; they may travel to Germany by using a valid passport only[9].

16 For nationals who require a Schengen visa, this is issued in the form of a type C Schengen visa. Since 2010, the business visa application procedure has been standardized for all Schengen countries.

Who decides if certain activities can be performed on a business visitor status?

17 In the case of those nationalities requiring a Schengen visa to enter for business purposes, the responsible embassy/consulate decides. For those nationalities who can travel on a visa waiver status, if unsure, one can contact an embassy or the local immigration authority in Germany to seek clarification.

Are 180-day periods based on the calendar year (e.g. January-June, July-December)?

18 No. The time period is not based on a calendar year. It is different for each traveler depending on their individual dates of entry and exit for non-visa nationals or the validity period of the Schengen visa for visa nationals.

Who monitors if 90 days in the 180-day period have been used up?

19 It is the responsibility of the traveler to keep track. The border police or, in some cases, the local German immigration office may check the days spent.

9 For a full list of countries requiring a Schengen visa for business or tourist travel, please refer to the following webpage http://www.auswaertiges-amt.de/DE/EinreiseUndAufenthalt/StaatenlisteVisumpflicht_node.html.

How can one prove how many of the 90 days in the 180-day period have been used up?

One can prove the number of days by the entry and exit stamps of the countries visited. 20

What happens if the 90 days within the 180-day period are exceeded?

If the allowed days have been exceeded, the stay is considered illegal and the traveler should leave the Schengen area immediately. 21

What can happen at border control when leaving the Schengen area if the 90 days have been exceeded?

The traveler may be held for questioning and a fine may be charged which needs to be paid on the spot. The amount of the fine is dependent on how many days have been exceeded. 22

Do business travelers who can travel without a Schengen visa need to carry any documents with them proving their purpose of stay?

No, there is no requirement. However, it might be helpful to have a letter from the company should clarification be needed at any time. 23

Which documents are necessary for a Schengen visa application?

In general these are: 24

- Valid passport;
- Application form;
- Biometric passport photo;
- Travel health insurance with a coverage of at least 30.000 Euro valid for the Schengen states;
- Round trip flight ticket;
- Invitation letter from Germany company;
- Employment confirmation from home company;
- Proof of sufficient means of subsistence.

The exact documents depend on the responsible German mission abroad and must be researched individually. 25

What is the standard processing time to obtain a Schengen visa?

26 The processing time for Schengen visa applications usually takes from 2 to 10 days. Due to the high workload at some embassies and consulates in certain countries, it can take several weeks to get an appointment for a visa application.

Can one travel to other Schengen countries with a Schengen visa issued by a German embassy/consulate?

27 Yes. Travel to other Schengen countries is allowed.

If travel is intended to several Schengen countries, at which country's embassy/ consulate should one file the Schengen visa application at?

28 The application needs to be filed at the diplomatic mission of the country that is the main travel destination (where the majority of time will be spent). If there is no main destination, the applicant must apply at the embassy/consulate of the country which will be the first port of entry.

Is the Schengen Visa always issued with the maximum duration of 90 days?

29 No. In general the first Schengen visa issued covers only the duration of the visitor's planed stay. For subsequent travel, the visa can be issued for a certain time frame with a restriction on the total allowed number of days (e.g. visa valid for three months but only allows a 30-day stay). Some Schengen visas are issued for several months or even up to one year or more. Despite the full validity period of the visa, the duration of stay is always limited to a maximum of 90 days within any 180-day timeframe.

Can a Schengen visa be extended in Germany?

30 No. A Schengen visa cannot be extended unless it is an emergency. German authorities typically consider health conditions which do not allow the individual to travel as an emergency. Should someone experience an emergency situation during his or her stay on a Schengen visa, contacting the local immigration office immediately is highly recommended.

Can one enter Germany multiple times with the same business visa?

31 Yes. If the visa is issued as a multiple entry visa, a visitor can travel in and out within the validity period of the visa as long as he or she does not exceed the allowed duration of stay noted on the visa.

What needs to be considered if one plans to spend vacation in the Schengen area before or after a business trip in Germany?

For non-visa nationals, the same travel status is used regardless of tourist or business purposes and so they are free to stay as long as they do not violate the 90 days within a 180-day rule. 32

For visa nationals, the type C visa will most likely be issued stating visitor/ business travel, however it is recommended to present any travel intentions to the embassy/consulate when applying for the visa. 33

What should a business traveler do if the purpose of stay changes to the need for a work permit?

The business traveler should contact their HR department to determine how to start a work permit process. Visa nationals will need to leave and apply for a visa for employment purposes, non-visa nationals should leave and re-enter once the new status is clarified or contact the local immigration office before the 90 days have been exceeded. 34

2. Process Overview for Achieving Immigration Compliance

If the reason of stay in Germany is not for a business visit as described in chapter II. 1. Business Travel, but it is clear that the individual will be performing tasks beyond the business travel description or will be taking up local employment or a temporary assignment then obtaining work permission is required. 35

This next section will aim to describe the general steps of the application process that need to be followed in order to obtain the final documentation allowing an employee to work and reside in Germany. In chapters 2.1 to 2.5 the application processes to be followed will be illustrated in detail. 36

The process to enter Germany for employment purposes is mainly determined by the nationality of the applicant. In order to meet immigration compliance, the following permits and documents are required and need to be secured: 37

Category of Nationals	Required permits/documents
EU/EWR nationals	Registration at local registration office only
Swiss nationals	Registration at local registration office, residence card (Aufenthaltskarte) for stays beyond 3 months
Non-visa nationals	Work permit, registration at local registration office, residence permit
Visa nationals	Work permit, long term national entry visa (type D), registration at local registration office, residence permit

38 While EU/EWR and Swiss nationals are exempt from the work permit requirement and only need to register at the local registration office (with the exception of Swiss nationals staying longer than 3 months), all other nationals are required to complete additional steps in order to live and work in Germany.

39 The typical steps that need to be followed are:

1. Work permit pre-approval application (Vorabzustimmung);
2. Long-term national entry visa application (visa nationals only) (Antrag auf Einreisevisum);
3. Address registration (Anmeldung);
4. Residence permit filing (Antrag auf Aufenthaltsgenehmigung);
5. Residence permit collection (Abholung der Aufenthaltsgenehmigung).

40 The work permit application needs to be filed at the Federal Employment Office (Bundesagentur für Arbeit). The department responsible for the processing and approval of work permission for foreigners is the International Placement Service (Zentrale Auslands- und Fachvermittlung (ZAV). All work permit applications Germany-wide are processed by 7 main teams located in Bonn, Duisburg (3 teams), Frankfurt am Main, Munich and Stuttgart[10].

41 In the past, the immigration process was started by involving the embassy or consulate (for visa nationals) or the local immigration office (for non-visa nationals) first and then the work permit was secured within this process. Since 2013 work permit pre-approvals can be obtained directly from the international placement service prior to involving the immigration authorities. This had an immensely positive impact on the complete processing time, shortening it considerably.

42 Some applicants may qualify for a work permit exemption (e.g. Blue Card – see chapter 3.4) in which case a pre-approval from the international placement service is not required.

43 In the case of visa nationals, upon obtaining the work permit pre-approval or determining that a work permit exemption applies, they must proceed to the responsible German mission abroad to file a long term national entry visa application. Upon receiving this document these nationals can enter Germany and start working immediately.

44 Non-visa nationals who have a work permit pre-approval or are exempt from the work permit requirement can enter Germany with their passports only on what is called a visa waiver status, but must complete the post arrival process in order to secure their permission to start working.

---

10 See: https://www.arbeitsagentur.de/web/content/DE/BuergerinnenUndBuerger/Arbeitund Beruf/ArbeitsJobsuche/ArbeitinDeutschland/Arbeitsmarktzulassung/Detail/index.htm?dfContent Id=L6019022DSTBAI531395.

The post arrival process for both visa and non-visa nationals includes address registration at the local registration office (Einwohnermeldeamt) and filing of the residence permit application at the local immigration office (Ausländerbehörde). 45

Since 2011, residence permits have been issued in a plastic card format, rather than a sticker in the passport as had been the case prior. The residence permit card (elektronischer Aufenthaltstitel) contains a chip inside it on which biometric data such as a photo and fingerprints are stored. In addition, personal data and information about the purpose of stay (i.e. employer, job title, family reunion etc.) are noted on this chip. Furthermore, a separate supplementary sheet is often issued which reflects the data on the chip in writing. 46

Due to the additional administrative time and effort required to process the cards (i.e. fingerprinting, printing of the card initiated at the central printing press in Berlin, coordinating additional appointments for collection of the cards), the high volume of applications and understaffed authorities, some immigration offices have temporarily reverted back to issuing the sticker permits in order to manage the work load. 47

Who files the work permit?

The work permit should usually be filed by the company (HR or recruitment department) hiring the employee, however a third party may also submit it on the company's behalf, or the applicants themselves can submit, however this is less common. 48

Does the person filing the application need to be officially authorized to do so?

Yes. If the person filing is not the applicant himself, then the application should be filed along with a power of attorney signed by the applicant. 49

Where is the application filed?

The work permit application is filed in Germany with the responsible team at the international placement services. 50

How is the responsible team at international placement services determined?

The responsible team at the employment office is determined by the location of the employing entity. Some work permit categories (i.e. intra-company exchange program, software or machinery implementation) are processed centrally at one specialized employment office, independent of the employing entity's location. 51

How is the work permit application filed?

52 The work permit is typically filed by email.

What are the standard documents required for a work permit?

53 The standard documents required for a work permit application are as follows but additional documentation such as translations can be requested at any time.
- Passport copy;
- CV;
- Copy of university degrees;
- ANABIN database excerpts (to prove equivalency of a foreign degree with a German degree);
- Local German work contract or assignment confirmation letter;
- Job description;
- Application form.

Do the original work permit documents need to be submitted?

54 No. Original documents do not need to be submitted. Scanned copies suffice.

Does the work permit application cost anything?

55 No. There are no fees charged in order to process the work permit application.

Does the applicant need to be present in Germany when the work permit application is filed?

56 No. The applicant does not need to be in country at the time of work permit filing.

Must the work permit be secured before travelling to Germany or can this be obtained after arrival?

57 For visa nationals, the work permit must be secured before they can receive an entry visa. Non-visa nationals can travel to Germany before the work permit is secured.

Is there a limit as to how long an approved work permit can be used?

58 Once a work permit is approved, the permit can be activated for up to 6 months after the issuance of the permit. So if a start date is postponed, the permit can still be used up to 6 months later.

How long is a work permit generally valid for?

The work permit is usually valid for the specific duration filed for which is commonly 1–2 years. In the case of an unlimited contract, the permit can be issued for up to 4 years and extended later. For certain work permit categories where the employee is only coming to Germany on a temporary assignment (personnel exchange program and international assignments), the permit can only be approved for a maximum of 3 years. 59

How far in advance can the work permit be filed?

There is no rule for how far in advance one may file the work permit. It can be filed several months in advance. 60

How far in advance should a work permit be filed?

It is recommended to file the work permit at least 12 weeks in advance in order to leave enough time for full processing. 61

In what form is the work permit issued?

The work permit pre-approval is issued as a regular sized piece of paper with the letterhead of the international placement services and a stamp. Once the residence permit is applied for and issued, the sticker permit or supplementary sheet (if issued as a residence permit card) will state the details of the approved employment on it. The residence permit then acts as both the residence and work permit in one document. 62

Does a cancellation of the work contract have an influence on the work permit?

If a work contract is terminated by either party, a work permit issued for a specific employer will lose its validity. The holder of the permit should contact the local immigration office in order to determine what effect contract termination has on the residence permit in general and if this could mean that they have to leave Germany. 63

Must changes in the employment parameters be communicated to the authorities and if yes, which authorities and when?

In all cases that are not permanent residency or limited residency with an unlimited work permit (where the work permit is not linked to a specific employer or job), changes in the employment parameters such as a change in employer, job title, promotion, change from an assignment to a local contract etc. should be communi- 64 cated as soon as possible to the local immigration office. At best this should be done before the change actually takes place.

Can the decision of the employment office be appealed?

65 As a constitutional state, Germany allows individuals the right to appeal decisions made by authorities. In the case of corporate immigration, it is doubtful whether legal action serves the purpose. Legal procedures against decisions made by the German authorities tend to be lengthy, and a change in outcome is often too late to be of use.

How is the embassy or consulate responsible determined?

66 The current place of residence outside of Germany determines the jurisdiction of application. Often, there is a strict division of consular jurisdiction, and applicants must provide proof of residence in the jurisdiction chosen. This can be satisfied by providing a driver's license, utility bills with an address in the jurisdiction, or similar documentation.

How is the immigration office responsible determined?

67 The immigration office is determined by the location of the address registered at the local registration office. Larger cities have their own or even several immigration offices, while smaller towns fall under the jurisdiction of an administrative district.

Must foreigners always carry the work and residence permit on him/her?

68 Foreigners must carry his residence permit with work authorization at all times. They must also carry a valid passport at all times. The residence permit does not replace the passport as an ID document.

What happens if the electronic residence permit gets lost or stolen?

69 If a permit gets lost or stolen, a police report must be filed. A new permit can be applied for with the police report and other supporting documents stated by the immigration office.

What happens if the passport gets lost or stolen?

70 If a passport gets lost or stolen a police report must also be filed and a new passport must be issued by the consulate or embassy of the issuing country. In the case of a sticker permit, a new one must be put into the new passport. In the case of an elec-

tronic residence permit, a new permit will also need to be printed as the permit is linked to a passport number.

Does the work/residence permit need to be cancelled when the individual leaves Germany prior to the expiry date of the permit?

One must de-register from the town hall when leaving Germany. The town hall will communicate the departure to the immigration office. A separate notification to the employment and/or immigration office is generally not required. 71

2.1 Address Registration

The registration at the local registration office (Einwohnermeldeamt) is mandatory for all individuals residing in Germany, independent of their nationality (even German citizens must register). While this is the only step that needs to be completed for EU/EEA nationals moving to Germany, the registration of a residential address is one of the crucial parts of the immigration compliance process for Non-EU/EEA nationals. 72

The local registration office is the public authority responsible for all registration law matters that, among other administrative duties, processes residence registration, re-registration to a new address within Germany (Ummeldung) and de-registration when leaving the country (Abmeldung). 73

With the German federal registration law (Bundesmeldegesetz) entering into force November 1st 2015, registration matters are now regulated consistently. 74

According to §17 of the German federal registration law, each individual has to register within two weeks of moving into a residence. The obligation to register, re-register and de-register an address is independent from the nationality of the individual. 75

Non-EU/EEA nationals need to register their address at the local registration office prior to their visit to the immigration office, as this determines the jurisdiction responsible for their application. 76

Since the implementation of the federal registration law, property owners are required to provide the tenant with a landlord confirmation (Wohnungsgeberbescheinigung) separate from the rental contract. This confirmation, as a minimum, needs to contain the name and address of the landlord, the address of the apartment and the name of each individual moving in. Additionally, the move-in or move-out date needs to be specifically mentioned on the landlord confirmation. Most local registration offices provide templates for the landlord confirmation, but these are not consistent throughout Germany. 77

How is the responsible local registration office determined?

78 The town hall responsible is determined by the location of the residence in Germany.

Are there more than one registration office in a jurisdiction?

79 Smaller towns will have only one registration office but larger cities may have several. Registration can be completed at any of the office locations in the city in question.

Must the registration be done in person or can it be done online?

80 The registration must be done in person but, in some jurisdictions this can be completed by an individual with a power of attorney signed by the person being registered and with the original passport. This should be clarified directly with the jurisdiction. At this time, registration cannot be completed online.

Can an appointment for registration be booked?

81 Most town halls nowadays either require an appointment for registration or at least give the opportunity to book an appointment. Especially in larger cities (e.g. Berlin, Hamburg. Frankfurt), it is highly **recommended or even mandatory** to book an appointment as going there without a booked appointment can include long waiting times or no processing at all. In the smaller jurisdictions, an appointment system is not often used and registration can usually be completed on a walk-in basis.

What address can be used for town hall registration?

82 The employee will need a residential address in Germany. This may be a long-term rental contract or a short-term serviced apartment.

Can one use a hotel or company address for registration?

83 Registration in a hotel is not usually possible, as they often refuse to sign the necessary landlord confirmation. A company address is not acceptable, since companies may not issue this confirmation.

Which documents are required for the registration?

84 Usually the original passport and the landlord confirmation are sufficient. However, if the individual is either accompanied by dependents (spouses and/or children) or wants to be registered as married, the marriage certificate and/or children's birth

certificates also need to be presented at the time of registration. Some registration offices will require the marriage and birth certificates to be translated into German. In very rare cases, these documents may also need to have a full legalization or apostille.

What needs to be done when the individual changes address within Germany?

When moving to a new accommodation, re-registration needs to be completed. This 85
process is the same as the first-time registration.

What needs to be done when the individual leaves Germany?

When leaving Germany, de-registration needs to be completed within two weeks of 86
departure.

2.2 EU/EEA and Swiss Nationals

From an immigration perspective, coming to Germany for employment purposes is 87
easiest for EU and EEA Nationals. EU Nationals enjoy freedom of movement rights within the European Union, which in Germany is regulated in the Act on the General Freedom of Movement for EU Citizens (Gesetz über die allgemeine Freizügigkeit von Unionsbürgern – Freizügigkeitsgesetz/EU – FreizügG/EU). According to §12 of that law, all EEA nationals also have the right of freedom of movement within the EU.

The right of freedom of movement means that EU and EEA nationals can enter 88
Germany at any time with their valid passport or national ID card and begin working immediately. The only step which needs to be completed upon arrival is the address registration (see chapter II. 2.1 Address Registration for details about the registration process).

Swiss nationals are handled slightly differently. Though not EU members, they 89
also have the right of freedom of movement in Germany and do not require a work permit. For stays under three months, they do not require a residence permit; however, if the stay will exceed three months, they need to apply for a special residence card for Swiss nationals (Aufenthaltserlaubnis-Schweiz).

What documents are required for EU/EAA and Swiss nationals to register an address in Germany?

For a general list of documents required for the city registry office registration, 90
please see chapter II 2.1.

Where does an applicant for the Swiss nationals' residence card apply?

91 The residence card is applied for at the immigration office responsible for the jurisdiction where the applicant is registered, where he or she is domiciled.

What documents are required for the Swiss national residence card?

92 The documents required can vary depending on the jurisdiction but commonly include:
- Passport;
- Biometric passport photo;
- Employment contract;
- Application form.

2.3 Non-visa Nationals

93 The immigration process for a non-visa national is largely post arrival, meaning that the individual will not need to apply for an entry visa at the German consulate/embassy in their home country or current country of residence before traveling to Germany.

94 The work permit pre-approval can be filed at any time. The applicant does not need to be present in Germany at the time of filing and is allowed to travel on business to Germany for a maximum of 90 days within a 180-day period while the application is in process. The applicant, however, is not allowed to perform work activities until the work permit has been approved and the post arrival steps of **address registration** and **residence permit** filing have been completed.

95 Once the **work permit** pre-approval is approved, the employee needs to travel to Germany (if not already there) and register their residential address at the town hall of the municipality in which they will reside in order to officially belong to the local jurisdiction. Only then will the immigration office for that jurisdiction take action in processing the residence permit.

96 Upon attending an appointment at the immigration office and successfully applying for the residence permit, the employee will receive a document which confirms their allowance to legally begin working. The final permit will be issued in the form of a sticker in the passport or as an electronic residence permit (**eAT**) which is a plastic card. The way the permit is issued (sticker vs card) depends on the jurisdiction and the work volume of the given office at that time.

97 Depending on the city the assignee/employee will live in, waiting times for an appointment can vary greatly. Thus, the sooner the employee can travel to Germany before the actual start date in order to complete the post arrival steps, the better the chances permission to work will be granted on time.

The steps for the immigration process for a non-visa national are as follows: 98

Pre arrival

- Work permit application – 2–3 weeks regular work permit; 1–3 weeks personnel exchange program

Post arrival

- Address Registration – 1 day;
- Residence permit filing – 1 day to file (but waiting times for appointments may be long – 1–5 weeks!);
- At this appointment the assignee should receive a temporary document allowing them to begin working*;
- Residence permit collection – 1 day (the permit is printed at the central printing press and can be collected 4–6 weeks after filing takes place).

Can the employee travel to Germany on a business visitor status while the work permit application is in process?

Yes, for 90 days within 180 days prior to work beginning. 99

When does the employee need to arrive in Germany to complete the post-arrival steps?

It is recommended to arrive in Germany at least a week or two before the employment/assignment begins in order to start the post-arrival formalities. 100

Can one schedule appointments at the authorities for completion of the post arrival steps?

Some authorities have appointment systems and appointments can be made by phone or online through the authority website. Other authorities do not have an appointment system and one must go to the regular opening hours and take a number. 101

What is the general waiting time to receive an appointment?

Registration office appointments can usually be secured on very short notice. In some immigration office jurisdictions, however, there can be a several week or even month wait to get an appointment. Often one must be registered at the town hall first before an immigration office appointment can be requested. 102

Which documents and in what form are required for the immigration steps?

103 For a general list of documents required for the work permit application please see chapter 3 – Most common permit types.

104 For a general list of documents required for the registration at the civil registry office please see chapter II 2.1. – Address Registration

105 The general documents required for the filing of the residence permit are:
- Valid passport for each applicant;
- Address registration confirmation;
- Apartment lease contract OR hotel/serviced apartment booking confirmation;
- Work contract or assignment confirmation letter (principal applicant);
- Work permit (ZAV) pre-approval (if applicable – principal applicant);
- Two biometric passport photos per applicant;
- Confirmation of health insurance;
- Fully completed and signed application form per applicant;
- Marriage certificate for spouse with a German translation;
- Birth certificates for children with a German translation;
- School confirmation for children above the age of six (6);
- Government Fee (Please see chapter II. 2.6 – Government Fees for the exact amounts).

106 The immigration authorities can request additional documents at any time. Some have authority specific templates they wish to have used. Often, translations of foreign language documents are required. Some jurisdictions also request the legalization of marriage or birth certificates which must be performed in the country of issuance. If required, this should be taken care of before the employee travels to Germany to avoid delays. For more information on legalization and apostilles on documents please see chapter 7.

What kind of health insurance is necessary for the residence permit application?

107 Health insurance can be an international insurance but must be comparable to German statutory health insurance. Employees with a local German employment contract automatically have access to the German health insurance system.

Can the employee change address during the immigration process?

108 Yes, but a change of jurisdiction while the permit is in process (i.e. from temporary to final accommodation in a different jurisdiction) can lead to confusion with authorities and delays in collecting the final permit, as the applicant's file will be transferred to the new jurisdiction in the middle of the process.

Is personal appearance required for any of the immigration steps?

Yes, all applicants above the age of 6 must file their residence permit in person at the immigration office. Some town halls require personal appearance for registration. 109

Can the employee sell their house/move their goods/prepare for final travel prior to work permit approval/visa issuance?

Selling your home/shipping goods and booking travel before the work permit is approved is not recommended and therefore at one's own risk. 110

2.4 Visa Nationals

Visa nationals require an entry visa issued by the German embassy or consulate located in their country of origin, or the country they are currently residing in, before coming to Germany for work. 111

To begin, work permit pre-approval needs to be applied for at the international placement services in Germany. Once issued, the original pre-approval needs to be sent to the applicant outside of Germany so that he or she can submit it along with other supporting documentation to the German embassy or consulate during the visa filing appointment. In some cases, if the applicant is clearly a Blue Card candidate,[11] the applicant can go straight to the visa filing appointment without a work permit pre-approval, and the embassy or consulate receiving the application has the power to decide directly on the issuance of the entry visa. In certain cases, the embassy will nevertheless involve the authorities in Germany (i.e. if the applicant has lived in Germany previously, is seeking self-employment and in some family reunion cases). 112

Once the visa has been issued, the employee can travel to Germany and begin working immediately. Address registration must take place within 2 weeks of finding long-term accommodation. Only after registration is complete will the local immigration office for that jurisdiction process the residence permit application and convert the visa into a final residence permit. 113

The steps for the immigration process for a visa national are as follows: 114

Pre-arrival steps
- **Work permit pre-approval application** (Vorabzustimmung) (Processing: 2–3 weeks)

11 In order to receive a Blue Card the applicant must hold a local contract, meet salary level requirements and have a university degree listed in the equivalency database – for more detail see the chapters on "Blue Card and Degree Recognition".

- **Visa application** (Antrag auf Einreisevisum)
  (Processing: 1 day to file and approximately 2–3 weeks for the visa to be issued)
  Once the entry visa is secured, the employee can enter Germany and begin working

Post-arrival steps
- **Address registration** (Processing: 1 day);
- **Residence permit application** (*Antrag auf Aufenthaltsgenehmigung*) (Processing: 1 day to file, but waiting times for an appointment can be up to 5 weeks);
- **Collection of the residence permit** (*Aufenthaltsgenehmigung*) (Processing: 1 day to collect, however the permit will be ready for collection only 3–6 weeks after the application has been filed).

Which documents and in what form are required for the immigration steps?

115 For a general list of documents required for the work permit application please see chapter 3 (Most Common Permit Types).

116 For a general list of documents required for the town hall registration please see chapter 2.1 (Address Registration).

117 For a general list of documents required for the residence permit application please see chapter 2.3 (Non-visa Nationals).

118 The most common documents for the visa application are listed below. These must be submitted as originals with two simple copies.
- Passport;
- Visa application form;
- Biometric passport photos;
- Resume/CV;
- Work contract or assignment letter;
- All university degrees (including excerpts from the German equivalency database);
- Proof of travel health insurance covering Germany;
- Original work permit pre-approval (if applicable);
- Government Fee (Please see chapter II. 2.6 – Government Fees for the exact amounts).

119 Each consulate/embassy will request additional documentation for the visa application (i.e. personal cover letter, copy of company registry, police clearance certificate, proof of accommodation in Germany etc.). Some of these will be country specific (i.e. the "Hukou" registry in China or the Russian employment book etc.). It is therefore always necessary to inquire about the application documents with the responsible German mission abroad.

In many cases, a German translation of documents is required. In some cases documents in English can be accepted, however this is not the norm. 120

In addition, some documents for the immigration process may require a stamp of authentication in the form of a legalization or apostille. For more information on this process please see chapter 8, Legalization/Apostille. 121

The authorities reserve the right to request additional documentation and translations at any time. 122

For how long is the entry visa issued by the Embassy/Consulate valid?

The visa issued by the embassy or consulate is usually valid for 3 months and gives the employee that amount of time to convert the entry visa into the final residence permit by completing the post-arrival steps. Issuance of the entry visa for 6 months can be implemented in busy phases where the immigration offices need additional time to allow for the timely scheduling of appointments for the residence permit application after arrival. 123

In cases where the planned full duration of stay in Germany does not exceed 12 months, one can request to have the visa issued for the full period and bypass the need to convert the visa into a residence permit upon arrival. This saves much time and effort for both the authorities and the employee. 124

How can a visa valid for the duration of up to 12 months be requested?

The visa application form includes a box that can be ticked if this request is to be made. 125

Can the employee retain/apply for a business visa while the work visa is in process?

The embassy/consulate reserves the right to cancel a Schengen visa issued by a German consulate once a work visa application has been filed. They can also refuse to issue a Schengen visa once a work visa application has been filed. 126

What is the reason for this?

Consulates are interested in avoiding having an employee travel to Germany and begin his or her job activities while travelling on a business status without a work permit. Therefore, this may, in some cases, restrict the applicant's ability to travel to Germany on business or for house-hunting purposes before the assignment or employment begins. 127

Can the employee travel to Germany while the work or visa application is in process?

128 There is no regulation in place restricting travel to Germany while work permits or visa applications are in process. However, the foreign national must have the proper authorization in place – either by virtue of nationality or necessary visa – to enter Germany on a business or tourist status. This can be either a Schengen visa or under the visa waiver program which applies to some of the visa nationals (Please see chapter II. 2. – Process Overview for achieving immigration compliance for information on this group of applicants).

When can a Visa national begin working?

129 The employee can start working immediately upon arrival with the work visa. If the visa does not cover the full duration of stay (maximum 12 months), this will be converted to a final residence permit during the post-arrival process.

Can the employee travel with a national work visa (category D) to other Schengen countries?

130 Yes, he or she may travel for business or tourist purposes to the other Schengen countries for up to 90 days within any 180-day period.

Is personal appearance required for any of the immigration steps?

131 Visa nationals need to file their work visas at the German embassy or consulate in person. After arrival, all applicants above the age of 6 must file their residence permit in person at the immigration office (Ausländerbehörde). In addition, some jurisdictions may require applicants to make a personal appearance at the town hall (Einwohnermeldeamt).

Can the employee sell their house/move their goods/prepare for final travel prior to visa issuance?

132 This is not recommended. Doing so is at one's own risk.

2.5 Renewal Process

133 The immigration offices recommend that the renewal process be initiated 12 weeks prior to the expiration of the current permit. This allows for renewal of the work permit with the employment office, personal appearance to file the renewal, fingerprinting and the printing of the new residence permit card at the central printing press.

Where capacity allows, some immigration offices will send a reminder or even schedule an appointment for filing the renewal application by post or email in advance. However, this is not often the case. The responsibility for timely renewal of the permit lies primarily with the applicant and secondarily with the employer, who should ensure that their employees have seamless permission to work during their stay in Germany. 134

As opposed to first time applications where one can file for a work permit pre-approval directly with the employment office, the work permit renewal application must be submitted to the immigration office in the jurisdiction where the foreign national is registered. The immigration office then forwards the application documents to the employment office or, respectively, assesses that the foreign national has been in Germany for 2 years already, and that his or her work permission no longer needs to be linked to a specific job. They may also check to see if the employer and the renewal of the residence permit can move forward without the involvement of the employment office. 135

Once the work permit has been approved, the foreign national then needs to visit the immigration office in person to submit any additional required documents and be fingerprinted. A new residence card is then ordered at the central printing press and, if required, a temporary permit is issued to bridge the gap between filing and issuance of the permit. 136

Does the employee need to leave Germany, or can he or she stay while the renewal is being processed?

The foreign national does not need to leave Germany at any time during the renewal process. If the old permit expires before the new final permit is issued, a temporary permit will be issued to bridge the gap, and the foreign national can continue to stay in Germany. 137

What is the latest date a renewal application can be filed?

The intent to renew the work and residence permits must be submitted no later than the last day the current permit is valid. 138

One thing to watch out for when a renewal application is submitted too late in the process and not enough time has been left to process the renewal of the work permit, the employee will retain the right to reside in Germany. However, some jurisdictions will make the employee stop working until the work permit portion of the process has been approved. This can be avoided by submitting the documents well enough in advance, usually within XYZ months of the permit's expiration date. 139

What if the renewal is not filed on time (i.e. the old permit has expired)?

140 Should an oversight occur and the residence permit expires, then the foreign national should reach out to the immigration office as soon as this has been discovered in order to file a renewal application. This demonstrates good intent, that it was an honest oversight and not done on purpose. In some cases a monetary fine may be charged.

What documents typically need to be submitted for the renewal?

141 As long as the renewal is simply an extension of the same job at the same conditions, the documents required for the work permit renewal are typically:

1. a renewal form;
2. the last three months' pay slips, to prove the salary payments stated in the original application were made;
3. an extension confirmation letter;
4. a new biometric passport photo;
5. proof of continued health insurance.

What if the employee has been promoted and earns a higher salary since the last application?

142 If the employee has only received a pay raise but his work activities and job title have not changed, nothing needs to be considered. If, however, a promotion has been given which changes the nature of the position being held, this needs to be communicated clearly. A new work permit approval may need to be applied for.

What if the employee has moved to a different jurisdiction than the one that issued the first work and residence permit?

143 As long as the employee re-registered his address with the Residents' registration office in the new jurisdiction when he or she moved, this should not be an issue. Once a foreign national moves to another jurisdiction the immigration office should be automatically informed and prompted to send the file to the immigration office in or responsible for the new jurisdiction.

What if the employee received a new passport in the meantime before the renewal?

144 If a new passport is obtained (i.e. the passport was full or lost or stolen and subsequently replaced), the foreign national should not wait for the renewal of the permit but contact the immigration office right away, since the residence permit card is linked to the current valid passport.

2.6 Government Fees

The applicable government fees for immigration matters can be found in chapter 3 of the Ordinance on Residence (Aufenthaltsverordnung). All fees need to be paid immediately (either in cash or with a bank card) at the respective authority (e.g. German embassy/consulate immigration office etc.) at times of filing the application. Fees paid at German embassies/consulates abroad must be paid in the local currency at the current exchange rate. The fees are valid for all nationalities, unless specifically stated. **145**

The most common government fees in 2016 for each step of the process include the following: **146**

1. Pre arrival
   - *Adult entry visa*: 60€ (to be paid in local currency at the embassy/consulate);
   - Entry visa for spouse of an EU national: No fee
2. Post arrival
   - *Address Registration*: No fee (Exception: A few jurisdictions, such as Hamburg, charge a fee of approximately 11€)
3. Work and residence permits
   - Work permit: no fee
   - *Temporary permit* (Fiktionsbescheinigung): 20€
   - *Adult Residence Permit* (including Blue Card):
     - Up to one year: 100€
     - Over one year: 110€
   - Residence permit for Turkish nationals:
     - 28.80€ for applicants 24 years and older
     - 22.80€ for applicants 24 years and younger
   - Residence permit for Swiss nationals:
     - 28.80€ for applicants 24 years and older
     - 22.80€ for applicants 24 years and younger
   - Permanent residence permit EU (Daueraufenthalt EG): 135€
   - Permanent residence (AKA Settlement) permit (Niederlassungserlaubnis): 250€
   - EU dependent permit:
     - 28.80€ for applicants 24 years and older
     - 22.80€ for applicants 24 years and younger
4. Renewals
   - Residence permit (including Blue Card):
     - Up to 3 months: 65€
     - Longer than three months: 80€
       Note: Fees for children under the age of 18 are 50% of the adult fee

3. Most common permit types

147 All individuals who are not EU/EEA or Swiss nationals need to obtain a work permit for Germany if they perform work activities in Germany.

148 There are numerous work permit types and each case has to be assessed individually since the work permit type depends on various factors, such as:
- educational background of the employee;
- whether local employment in Germany is intended;
- whether an employee is a company specialist or executive;
- length of assignment/work agreement;
- previous employment with an entity of the company outside Germany.

149 The most common permit types listed below will be described in more detail in the following chapters:
- International Agreements, §29 (5) BeschV;
- Intra-Company Exchange Program (§10 BeschV);
- Employment of certain nationals (§26 BeschV);
- Blue Card EU (§§19a AufenthG, 2 (1), (2) BeschV);
- Permit for University Graduates (§2 (3) BeschV);
- Executives and Specialists (§§3; 4 BeschV);
- Training Permit (§17 AufenthG);
- Permit for Software/machinery implementation (§19 BeschV);
- Van der Elst (§21 BeschV).

3.1 International Agreements (§29 (5) BeschV)

150 Work permission based on section 29 (5) of the Employment Regulation (*Beschäftigungsverordnung* or, more commonly *BeschV*) focuses on the implementation of international agreements based on the provision of services. These services are regulated through General Agreements in Services (GATS) or other free trade agreements.

151 Individuals employed by a foreign company based outside of Germany who are being assigned to work at a German entity of that company or at a client site can be granted work permission for a limited period of time.

152 Practical experience shows that authorities are making use of this rule quite frequently, as it covers a large population of assignees.

What countries fall under GATS or any other free trade agreements?

153 The majority of countries are member of GATS or another free trade agreement. The exact list is on the WTO webpage, https://www.wto.org/english/thewto_e/whatis_e/tif_e/org6_e.htm.

The number of countries not having any free trade agreement and therefore are not eligible for this permit type are so minimal that it does not have practical relevance. 154

What is the maximum duration allowed for this permit?
The maximum duration an employee can stay on this type of permit is 36 months. 155

What happens once the maximum duration has been reached?
If the individual needs to stay beyond 36 months, the German entity needs to offer him or her a local German employment contract and the permit type needs to be changed. 156

Are there any prerequisites that must be fulfilled?
The employee must be employed at the entity outside of Germany for at least 12 months prior to the assignment in Germany. There must be an entity of the company in Germany, even if they are placed at a client site. 157

What kind of employment contract is required?
Secondment contract. This permit can only be issued if the employee remains on home contract and does not receive a local employment contract with the German entity. 158

Is there a minimum salary requirement?
The foreign employee must earn the same salary as a German employee with similar qualification and performing the same job. 159

What kind of allowances can be taken into account when calculating the minimum salary?
Allowances which are paid as a monthly lump sum for the employee's choice of purpose can be taken into consideration. For example, payments against receipts (expense payments) or direct payments of housing rent by the employer to the landlord cannot be used. The employees must receive the allowances in such a fashion that allows them to use them at their discretion. 160

Does the individual need university degree?

161 No. This permit can be granted to employees who do not hold a university degree.

Are there any restrictions with this permit type?

162 Yes. The holder of this type of permit does not qualify for **child allowance payments** by the German government. For more information, see the chapter on social security.

3.2 Intra-Company Exchange Program (§10 BeschV)

163 Much like the international agreement permit, the intra-company exchange program is intended for employees of an internationally acting company who will be **seconded** to an entity of the same company in Germany. It is a simplified process that waives the German labor market check, requires less intensive paperwork and is usually approved within a shorter space of time (1–2 weeks). Companies that wish to benefit from this program must first register their company with international placement services. The term "international exchange program" (**internationaler Personalaustausch**) implies that an exchange takes place. One of the requirements for registration is a list of Germany-based employees who have left Germany on assignment. This list indicates how many employees a company has sent out, and it is in relation to this number that the employment office can allow foreign employees to enter on this type of permit. In short: For every Germany-based employee you send out of Germany, you may bring one foreign employee in.

How does a company register for this program?

164 This can be done by:

- submitting information on the company (usually, providing the company website suffices);
- submitting information on related entities (entities are those subsidiaries with a share ownership of at least 50%);
- providing a list of German based employees who have been sent outside of Germany on assignment for at least three months within the last three years.

Does this registration need to be renewed at any time?

165 Yes. The company should make sure to update their list of outbound assignees on at least a yearly basis in order to ensure the available contingency remains up to date.

If the company does not send Germany-based employees out of Germany, can they still register for this program?

No. In order to be able to register you must provide a list of employees who have left Germany on assignment, where they went to and for how long. Even if you only have one employee, you can still register and then have one spot open to allow one foreigner in. 166

What happens if all exchange spots are used up?

If the full contingency has been used up, you can submit an updated list of employees who have left Germany on assignment to gain more spots. If no further employees have gone, the company will need to wait until they have assigned an employee to work outside of Germany before they can use this permit type again. 167

What if an assignee ends his assignment early but his permit is still valid?

If an assignee leaves Germany earlier than expected, the employment office can be informed and the time can be booked back to the open contingency. 168

Must the assignee be physically located at a subsidiary of the company or can he/she be situated at a client site in Germany?

The assignee can be located at a client site, but an entity in Germany must sponsor the work permit application. 169

What is the maximum duration allowed for this permit?

The maximum duration an employee can stay on this type of permit is 36 months. 170

What happens when the maximum duration is used up? Is the assignee not allowed to extend his/her stay?

For some nationalities, such as non-visa nationals, a different permit category may be relevant (e.g. §26 BeschV – see chapter 3.3). For others, such as visa nationals, the switch to a local German contract may be a solution. One can apply for the international personnel exchange a second time if they have spent the same amount of time that they were in Germany outside of it again. After this absence, they would be eligible to apply again. 171

Does the assignee need to have been employed by the company outside Germany for a specific amount of time in order to qualify?

172 No. Previous employment at an entity of the company abroad is not required.

Are there any specific requirements in order to qualify for this permit type?

173 The applicant must have a university-level degree (however, this does not need to be listed in the German degree recognition database as it does with some other permit types), or the employee must have a considerable amount of work experience with the company abroad. In addition the salary (including allowances) must match the salary a German employee earns with similar qualifications and in a similar position. There is no set salary minimum. Should the employment office think it is too low, they may request to see the work contract of a comparable German employee with the same salary level.

What kind of allowances can be taken into account when calculating the minimum salary?

174 Allowances, which are paid as a monthly lump sum for the employee's choice of use, can be taken into consideration. For example, payments against receipts (expense payments) or direct payments of housing rent by the employer to the landlord cannot be used. The employees must receive the allowances to be used at their disposal.

Are there any specific contractual requirements?

175 This permit type can either be applied for
- if the assignee remains a full employee of the home company;
- if the host company signs a limited employment contract with the assignee and the home company issues a letter confirming the assignees right to return.

Are there any restrictions with this permit type?

176 Yes. The holder of this type of permit does not qualify for **child allowance payments** by the German government. For more information, see the chapter on social security.

3.3 Employment of certain nationals (§26 BeschV)

177 Based on §26 BeschV (Beschäftigung bestimmter Staatsangehöriger), the International Placement Services can give their approval to certain nationalities for taking up any type of employment. This approval is limited to individuals from:

- Andorra
- Australia
- Canada
- Israel
- Japan
- Monaco
- New Zealand
- San Marino
- South Korea
- United States

The applicant needs a binding job offer with an employer in Germany and a labor market check must be performed. The labor market check is performed by the local employment office in the jurisdiction of the host company. During this process they will check that there is not already a German or other EU citizen actively seeking work in Germany who is qualified to do this job and that the salary is comparable to a German national performing the same job. There is no charge for the labor market check. NOTE: Under German law, foreign workers may not be paid less than a German national with the same qualifications to perform a job in Germany. 178

An advantage of this category is that the eligibility for this permit type is independent of the contractual set-up of the employment. This can be used for either international assignments (with an assignment contract from the home company or for individuals who are hired locally in Germany). 179

An additional advantage of this category is that the applicant's university degree demonstrating his or her qualifications for the position does not have to be listed in the degree equivalency database (for more information see chapter on Degree Equivalency). 180

Since January 1st, 2016, there is a new employment category available for nationals of Albania, Bosnia Herzegovina, Kosovo, Macedonia, Montenegro and Serbia (§26 Abs. 2 BeschV). For these additional nationalities, easier access to the German labor market has been implemented. There is no restriction on certain professions and special qualifications do not need to be proven. This category is only available until the end of 2020. 181

As these West Balkan States are considered safe countries of origin and asylum applications from these nationals have a limited chance of being approved, this new category gives them an alternative opportunity to apply for a work and residence permit for Germany. The approval, however, may not be issued to those applicants who have, within the 24 months before application, received benefits under the Asylum Seekers Benefits Act. 182

Note: This ban does not apply to those who applied for asylum between 1 January 2015 and 24 October 2015, were still in Germany on 24 October 2015 and then left the country immediately. 183

184 This permit type covers a wide range of assignment types and activities and is versatile, allowing easier access to the labor market for these nationals.

What is the maximum duration allowed for this permit?

185 There is no maximum duration for this permit type. Additionally, it can be renewed if the individual continues to stay in Germany.

How long does a labor market check take?

186 The duration of the labor market check varies depending on the position and location. Generally, however, this permit type is usually approved within 2–4 weeks.

3.4 Blue Card EU (§19a AufenthG)

187 With the introduction of the Blue Card EU in 2012, the German government implemented the EU directive 2009/50/EG and followed the aim to increase the migration of highly qualified workers in Germany.

188 With the Blue Card EU, highly qualified, non-EU citizens can receive work permission for any employment adequate to their qualification. The requirements for the issuance of a Blue Card EU are a:
- German or foreign university degree considered equivalent to a German degree;
- local German employment contract;
- minimum annual gross salary for "scarce occupations" (Mangelberufe).

189 The minimum annual gross salary in 2016 is 49,600 EUR for regular occupations and 38,688 EUR for scarce, or understaffed, occupations. The minimum salaries are based on the social security contribution ceiling (Beitragsbemessungsgrenze in der allgemeinen Rentenversicherung) and at the end of each calendar year are published for the following year.

190 When the applicant initially applies for his or her Blue Card EU it is issued with a maximum duration of 4 years for instances where a permanent employment contract exists. In cases where the employment contract is limited in time (under four years), the Blue Card EU will be issued for the duration of the employment contract plus an additional three months.

191 The process of obtaining a Blue Card EU is similar to the usual process for employment purposes. However, this category represents a work permit exemption and a work permit pre-approval is not required. In the case of scarce occupations where there is a shortage of specialists, the approval from the local employment office in Germany will be sought only in order to ensure that the applicant does not earn less than a German citizen would earn for doing the same job. For all other applications,

those with the higher minimum salary, the decision to issue a Blue Card EU can be made by either the German embassy or consulate abroad. This is the case for all Visa nationals applying for an entry visa. Other applicants still see their application decision rendered by the local immigration office in Germany, as is the case for all non-visa nationals arriving on their passports only.

What payments can be calculated to reach the minimum salary?

All guaranteed payments can be calculated to reach the minimum salary. If bonus 192
payments are contingent upon job performance, they cannot be taken into consideration.

If the minimum salary to receive a Blue Card is raised at the beginning of each year, does this have an impact on existing Blue Cards?

A minimum salary rise would not impact previously issued Blue Cards. The new sal- 193
ary level of the year in question would only need to be considered if the employee changes employers and the change needs to be confirmed by the immigration office.

What are the scarce occupations?

Scarce, or understaffed, occupations are those classified in groups 21, 25 and 221 of 194
the International Standard Classification of Occupations (ISCO). The most common occupations currently include engineers, IT specialists, medical doctors, mathematicians and natural scientists.

Can one change the employer on an existing Blue Card?

After two years the restriction to working for the employer which you were working 195
for at the time the Blue Card was issued, is no longer applicable. Within the first two years, the holder of the Blue Card EU needs to inform the immigration office responsible of any change of employer.

How can someone determine if his or her foreign university degree is considered equivalent in Germany?

All equivalent degrees are listed in the database Anabin. For further information on 196
degree equivalency, see chapter II. 5. – Degree Equivalency.

Can a visa national enter Germany on a Schengen visa (type C) and apply for a Blue Card?

197 No. All visa nationals have to apply for an entry visa (type D) at the foreign diplomatic post (e.g. consulate).

Does the Blue Card EU issued in Germany also allow work in other EU member states?

198 No. As with any other German residence permit, the Blue Card EU allows the holder to travel within the Schengen states without an additional visa for a maximum of 90 days within 180 days. The purpose of this travel is limited to business and tourist activities and does not automatically allow employment in the other EU country. When holding any German residence permit, including the Blue Card and planning to work in another EU member state, the requirements to work in that country need to be checked.

Can my family get a Blue Card?

199 Blue cards can only be issued to applicants who meet all of the following criteria:
- receive a local German employment contract;
- earn a certain amount of salary;
- have a degree listed in the database Anabin.

Family members do not receive a Blue Card.

What are the benefits of a Blue Card?

200 The benefits of a Blue Card are that:
- approval can be given more quickly, since the embassy or immigration office; can, in most cases, approve without the involvement of the International Placement Services;
- one is eligible to file for permanent residency faster, as early as after 2 years if all other requirements are met;
- spouses are exempt from needing to provide proof of knowledge of the German language before coming to Germany;
- the Blue Card EU holder and his family can leave Germany for a maximum of 12 months without the risk of losing the German residence permit.

3.5 Foreign university graduates (§2 (3) BeschV)

In certain cases, applicants are given a local contract and have a foreign university degree that is considered comparable to a German university degree. Nevertheless, their salary level does not meet the minimum requirement for the issuance of a Blue Card. In these cases, a permit can still be issued, but the holder does not benefit from the Blue Card status (i.e. permanent residency cannot be applied for more quickly). 201

Could such an applicant get a regular Blue Card at some point?
Only if their salary is raised to meet the requirements for a Blue Card. 202

3.6 Executives and Specialists (§§3; 4 BeschV)

According to §3 BeschV, a work permit without the approval from the International Placement Services can be given to executives (Führungskräfte). Executives in this context are individuals on the upper management levels within the company. 203

In particular, executive managers (Leitende Angestellte), as defined by the works constitution act (§5 Abs. 3 Betriebsverfassungsgesetz), who are granted proxy (Prokura) or general power of attorney rights (Generalvollmacht) receive work permission based on this legal clause. 204

The criteria defining executive managers is very strict. People assigned to these roles must, amongst other requirements, have the authority to make personnel decisions. This legal basis can be used for executive managers from a company outside of Germany with an executive position that is important for the development of the company. 205

Based on §4 BeschV, the approval from the International Placement Services can be given for executive managers and other experienced employees with special company knowledge. These company specialists are individuals that have special expert knowledge essential for the business' German operations. The company specialists must have special knowledge and experience in their area of expertise, which is generally based on their previous work experience. 206

The special knowledge and experience can be proven by the individual's CV showing their professional career and education certificates proving their qualifications. The paid salary level is also an indicator for the required level of expertise. The salary these individuals need to receive must be significantly higher than what a regular German employee would earn. 207

A need-based labor market check will not be performed for the approval based on §3 or §4 BeschV. 208

Both paragraphs are only used in cases where the special knowledge, work experience and management level can be proven to the authorities. 209

Is there a defined salary level for executives and specialist?

210 There is no minimum salary level as such, and the authorities involved in the expat approval process (i.e. International Placement Services and immigration office) will assess each individual case. They salary payments and the required level usually differ and depend on the commercial sector and the occupation.

How can one prove he or she is a proxy of the German company?

211 The individual needs to prove he or she is an official proxy by submitting an extract from the commercial registry (Handelsregisterauszug) of the German company.

What is the maximum duration allowed for this permit type?

212 There is no maximum duration.

3.7 Training Permit (§17 AufenthG)

213 Short-term training of a company's employees for a period of under 90 days within 12 months is covered by a Schengen business status. With just their passports, non-visa nationals may travel to Germany to participate. Visa nationals can file for and receive a Schengen visa (type C) by submitting a written training plan, along with the other application documents, to allow them to travel for this purpose.

214 Sometimes employees need to go abroad for a longer period of time to another entity of a company to be trained in certain skills or gather know how (AKA: a know–how transfer), which they can then apply to their daily work once they return to their home country. Such training is important for sustaining and expanding knowledge and, in some cases, even necessary for promotions.

215 Some companies also offer graduate or global graduate programs, which introduce recent graduates to various areas within a company and send them on rotation to different entities world-wide to gather work, company-related and international experience. These programs usually range from a period of 1–2 years and require intensive organization to obtain the correct work permission for each rotation country at the right time.

216 For these situations a training permit would apply. This type of permit specifically requires the submission of a detailed training plan covering the duration of stay.

Which documents are required for this type of work permit?

217 Among the regular work permit documents, this type of permit specifically requires the submission of a training plan. This training plan should be drawn up on a

month-by-month or week-by-week basis, describing the training topic to be covered and naming a supervisor for each area. In some cases the supervisor is always the same person or the same activities are performed for several weeks in a row, with on-the-job training being the main method. No matter how the training is set up, some idea of the rundown detailing how the training will move forward should be provided.

Is there a maximum duration for which this permit type can be issued?

This permit can be approved for the duration of the structured training plan covering the topics necessary for reaching established training goals. 218

Can this permit type be extended?

Yes, however, the employment office reserves the right to examine whether the purpose of stay has been successfully achieved and whether an extension is necessary. 219

Can an employee who is in Germany on a training permit (i.e. Global Graduate program) transfer to a full employee status?

Yes, if, following the training period, the employee is offered a regular employment contract with the company in Germany. It is, however, not always possible for the employee to change his or her status from a training permit to an employment permit while remaining in Germany. A passage in the law text requires at least visa nationals to leave Germany and re-enter with an employment visa issued by the German embassy or consulate making a seamless continuation of activity difficult. 220

Does this type of permit enable a foreign employee to give or perform training?

Yes, for stays under 90 days within a 12-month period. If an employee is coming for a longer period to give training, a regular work permit needs to be applied for. 221

Can trainees be paid a lower salary than a full employee?

No, a trainee may not be employed at less favorable conditions than a comparable German national. As a rule, at least an entry-level salary for the respective job category must be paid. 222

3.8 Permit for software/machinery implementation (§19 BeschV)

223 In some cases, an employee needs to visit a client site in Germany in order to install, mount/demount, service, repair, or instruct in the use of machines or software data programs which have been purchased from the company. It is in fact only logical that an employee from the selling company needs to come to Germany during the initial phase to install/mount the product and teach client-company employees how to use it properly. Or, if at a later time the product becomes defective or needs servicing, the foreign employee of the seller needs to visit the client to repair it. As far as a work permit in this category is concerned, submitting proof of a purchase order for the product is crucial.

224 Implementation activities of this sort are considered exempt of international placement services approval if the duration of stay does not exceed 90 days within a 12-month period. Nevertheless, a statement must be made at the employment office through a special template form listing:

- employee names, nationalities, duration etc. ;
- additional supporting documents;
- purchase order of the machine/data program;
- description of tasks;
- passport copy of relevant employees.

225 Processing takes approximately 3 business days and the confirmation that notification has been given to the employment office is sent by e-mail. With this confirmation, the employee – visa or non-visa nationals – can then file his or her entry visa at their nearest German mission abroad. The visa is issued fairly quickly in the form of a Type C Schengen visa – with the addition of the purpose of stay – and can be issued usually within 1–2 weeks after filing.

226 For employees being deployed to Germany longer than 90 days and up to 3 years, a long-term work and residence permit can be applied for within this legal framework. This requires a regular work permit approval, not just notification at the employment office. Processing times for the work permit approval and the visa processing, in the case of a visa national, are considerably longer (4–8 weeks). Non-visa nationals staying longer term for this purpose do not need to apply for an entry visa (see section 2.2).

Are the notification and work permit applications submitted to the same employment office as for other work permit types?

227 No, the employment office in Stuttgart handles all applications of this nature for the whole of Germany.

What if the employee(s) must travel very quickly to Germany and notification is not made to the employment office?

Situations arise where, for example, a product requires repair and time was not **228** taken to properly follow compliance rules, such as notifying the employment office of the need for travel. In cases where employees coming to Germany for product implementation (or repair) purposes have not submitted the requisite notification to the employment office, the employees are considered to be in breach of German law. This may bring about consequences, such as a monetary fine.

Are consulting services purchased from a company also considered under this legal basis?

Consulting services purchased from a company do not fall under this category. If **229** providing this type of service, alternative work permit categories need to be explored.

3.9 Van der Elst Visa (§21 BeschV)

Europe, with its many countries located in close proximity to each other, presents **230** an interesting geographic situation for companies that often require the deployment of an employee to several EU countries at once for work purposes. Immigration in Germany has unfortunately not yet caught up to this trend, and an EU-wide work permit does not yet exist. This leaves companies little flexibility to have non-EU employees work at several related entities or clients within Europe.

One EU-based development in this direction, however, was the introduction of **231** the Van der Elst visa. This visa is one step towards facilitating the distribution of the non-EU workforce throughout the EU countries. In short, it is a work permit "exemption" for third country nationals who are already in possession of a work and residence permit for one EU country and who need to temporarily come to Germany to work at a client site. For example, company X based in the UK has an Indian employee who has the skills required on a project at a client site in Germany. This visa type will allow a relatively quick approval to cover the company's needs because it allows entry to work in Germany based on the fact that the employee already has a work permit in the first EU country. It is to be noted, however, that the work must be performed at a client site at which the employee is rendering a service and not a branch of the same company.

This type of visa is a purely consular process which means that the embassy/ **232** consulate decides on their own whether all requirements are fulfilled and if the visa can be issued. The local authorities within Germany (employment or immigration offices) are not involved in the process. This makes the process quite quick, allowing the non-EU employee to travel to and work in at least a second EU country within a relatively short space of time.

Which documents are required for this type of visa?

233 Requirements can vary in different countries, but are commonly:

- Application form;
- Two biometric passport photos;
- Original passport;
- Residence permit with long enough validity to allow the assignee to return to the first EU country;
- Copy of the employment agreement with company in first EU country;
- Confirmation from the company providing the services (first EU country) with full name, birth date, birth place, passport number of the employee, confirming the current employment of the assignee in first EU country, the begin and end of the duration of stay in Germany, location and address of the client site in Germany, short description of the services to be performed in Germany at the client site;
- A letter of support from the company in Germany;
- Sufficient health insurance covering Germany for the duration of stay (international health insurance covering Germany).

How long can the visa be issued for?

234 The visa can be issued for up to 12 months.

Can the visa be extended?

235 Yes, the visa can be extended, however the holder must leave Germany and reapply for a new visa at the German mission abroad, then re-enter again.

Can the employee be sent on a project to a branch of the same company or must this be a client site?

236 In general, in order to qualify for the van der Elst, the employee needs to be visiting a client site to render services. In some cases, if the employee is going to work on a specific project being executed in the second EU country (host) but the project is headed by the first EU country (home) then an exception can be made. If the project is being headed by the host country and for lack of own employees they borrow from another EU country then a personnel exchange situation exists and not a Van der Elst situation.

How long does it take to receive the visa?

The visa should be issued within approximately one to two weeks of filing the application. 237

3.10 Self-Employed Status (§21 AufenthG)

Foreigners may also settle in Germany as self-employed entrepreneurs (§21 AufenthG – Selbstständige Tätigkeit). In order to qualify for this type of permit: 238

1. There must be a certain level of economic interest or a regional need in Germany.
2. The activities must have a positive effect on the German economy.
3. The applicant must have secure financing for their endeavors through personal capital or a loan.

These requirements will be checked by the local immigration office in the jurisdiction where the individual plans to live. In order to assess these points, the immigration office will involve, for example, the local Chamber of Industry and Commerce (IHK – Industrie und Handelskammer), whose specialists in the respective area of business will thoroughly examine the business plan, the viability of the business idea and financials.[12] If the Chamber of Industry and Commerce issues a positive report, the immigration office can usually approve the permit immediately after all other requirements are fulfilled. 239

In addition to the approval from the trade and industry authorities responsible, some of the other documentation that needs to be submitted includes: 240

- a CV;
- university degrees and proof of other work-related qualifications;
- proof of sufficient health insurance;
- proof of living space.

A background check will be initiated by the immigration office prior to granting the permit to ensure that the foreign national has no criminal record, or is not under any ongoing criminal investigations. This security screening usually takes 3–4 weeks. 241

Visa nationals will need to file for an entry visa at the local German mission abroad. That embassy or consulate will seek the involvement of the local immigration office, who in turn involves the Chamber of Industry and Commerce and other competent authorities. With so many parties involved, the process can take several weeks to months to be completed. 242

12 Where possible, necessary, or both, additional authorities will be involved in the decision making process.

243 Non-visa nationals can submit the documentation directly to the local immigration office. The security check and communication with the trade and industry authorities will also take place so that the processing time for this type of permit also stretches over several weeks.

Why are the local chamber of commerce (IHK) or other business and trade authorities involved in the approval process?

244 The chamber of commerce and other authorities are involved because the Immigration office does not have the background knowledge or specialization to assess the business concepts and plans of freelance business people. This needs to be examined by professionals who have knowledge of the business.

What type insurance is required for the immigration process?

245 Proof of health insurance needs to be submitted for all applicants. Individuals applying for this type of permit who are over the age of 45 may only be issued a residence permit if they also have a sufficient retirement/pension plan.

Is there a limit to the term of this type of permit?

246 Yes. This permit can be issued for a term of 3 years maximum, after which time a permanent residence permit can be issued if the individual has successfully completed the setting up of his or her business in Germany and is able to finance him- or herself and any accompanying family members through adequate income.

What if the individual has not successfully carried out the activities and is unable to finance him- or herself through income generated by the self-employment?

247 If the immigration office has determined that the individual has not met the financial goals as outlined in the business plan, unless there is another legal basis upon which to issue a residence and work permit, the individual will need to leave Germany.

Is the International Placement Services (Zentrale Auslands- und Fachvermittlung – ZAV) involved in the application process?

248 As self-employment is not considered employment as defined by the Social Security Code (Sozialgesetzbuch – SGB IV), the involvement of the International Placement Services is not required in the decision making process. However, the immigration office has the right, in case of doubt, to request assistance from the International Placement Services and will decide to do so on a case-by-case base.

4. Eligibility for permanent residency

Permanent residency, an unlimited work and residence permit for Germany, allows the holder the same rights as a German national has (e.g., work without a work permit, unemployment benefits, with the exception that they are not allowed to vote in federal elections). Holders of this permit do not need to inform the immigration office of a job change. The permit is issued until the expiry date of the passport and can be issued again with very minimal documentation once a new passport has been obtained. If the holder leaves Germany for more than six months at one time, however, the permit will become invalid unless a certificate of return (Rückkehrberechtigung or Nichterlöschensbescheinigung), is secured beforehand, something that should be done whenever possible. The word permanent is therefore somewhat misleading. German residence permits are always linked to actual long term residency in Germany and do not continue to remain in force once you leave the country for longer periods. 249

Permanent residency remains an option, and may be obtained in various ways.

4.1 Permanent Residency after 5 years of legal residency in Germany (Niederlassungserlaubnis, §9 AufenthG; Daueraufenthalt-EU §9a)

This method is the longest method but gives the option for permanent residency even if the applicant is not considered a highly qualified applicant with university level education. 250

A foreigner can obtain permanent residency if: 251

- He/she has held a valid residence permit for Germany for the last five years;
- He/she has enough financial means to finance his- or herself;
- He/she has paid into compulsory or voluntary pension plan in Germany for at least 60 months;
- He/she can prove knowledge of the German language and of the German legal, political, cultural and social norms. This is proven through the successful completion of the integration course offered by the federal office for migrants and refugees.

Alternatively, there is a long-term residency permit based on EU law. Called an EC long-term residence permit (Daueraufenthalt-EU), it is issued in a very similar way. The title, however, is misleading, as many think that this permit gives them not only permanent German residency, but also permission to work in all EU countries. This is, however, not the case. If one holds the equivalent of the EC long-term residence permit in one EU country (e.g. Austria) and then moves to Germany to live and work, the worker still needs to apply with the German authorities for permission to work, live, or both in Germany. On the other hand, the EC long-term residence permit does 252 facilitate immigration from one EU country to another by, for example, exempting visa nationals holding the permit from the need of an entry visa from the mission abroad. That is, these permit holders may travel into Germany on their long-term permit and complete the steps locally, thereby easing the work permit requirements process in the new EU country.

4.2 Research Scientists and Professors (§19 AufenthG (2))

253 These occupations are considered highly qualified and justify the immediate issuance of permanent residency without a labor market check. Until July 2013 other occupations such as Managing Directors and employees earning a high salary could obtain this permit. This was reduced to include only academic scholars with specialized areas of expertise and university professors, teaching staff or academic personnel with specialized work experience.

4.3 Blue Card holders (§19a AufenthG)

254 The Blue Card allows holders to apply for permanent residency more quickly than those issued a regular work and residence permit. One can file for permanent residency after:

- 33 months in country, with proof of payment contributions into the German social security plan and with at least A1 level German language skills;
- 21 months in country, with proof of payment contributions into the German social security plan and with at least B1 level German language skills.

255 The level of language competency is based on the Common European Framework of Reference for Languages. More details on that assessment can be found online at: https://ec.europa.eu/eusurvey/files/8a87d2f5-aba8-4272-b8f1-4922fe12c425.

4.4 Other methods of obtaining permanent residency

256 Next to the beforementioned ways (please see chapters 4.1, 4.2, 4.3) there are additional ways of obtaining permanent residency within a shorter span of time. These are:

- Being a graduate of a German university (§18b AufenthG)
  With a German university diploma, one may apply after 2 years of residency in Germany. The requirements are:
  - a German university degree;
  - a job offer in the academic field of the degree;

  - proof of payment into the social security program in Germany for the 24 months prior.
- *Being self-employed* (§21 (4) AufenthG)
  One can apply for permanent residency after three years if the business plan has been realized and the individual can support herself/himself financially.
- Being married to a German citizen (§28 (2) AufenthG)
  Individuals married to a German citizen can apply for permanent residency, if:
  - they had a residence permit in Germany for at least 3 years;
  - the family unity still continues;
  - the foreign individual is able to speak what authorities consider a sufficient level of German, which is usually B1.

5. Degree Equivalency

The 2012 introduction of the Blue Card placed a significant focus on the question of 257
foreign university degree equivalency to those awarded by Germany institutions. Until this time, and for some permit types still today, a simple copy of the degree certificate was sufficient.[13] For any type of permit falling under §2 of the employment law act (BeschV), degree equivalency has become a crucial part of the work permit process. This process is of much importance, as this type of permit is one of the most common permit types issued for employees receiving a local work contract in Germany.

The employment office responsible is able to issue work permit pre-approvals 258
for most work permit categories prior to the application for an entry visa (visa nationals) or residence permit (non-visa nationals). Until 2016, this was also possible in regards to Blue Card applications and was a guideline for embassies and local immigration offices to issue this type of permit. This gave the applicant and employer some kind of reassurance that the aspired permit category is considered acceptable before the residence application process was started.

The embassies and local immigration offices, however, also have the authoriza- 259
tion to decide directly on Blue Card applications. This is one of the few permit types that can be issued by these authorities without the involvement of the local employment office. A large part of this process is to determine the degree equivalency to a German degree. It appears that differences in opinion between the employment office pre-approvals and the judgement of the embassies or local immigration offices have led to some disagreement.

13 Whether or not a German-language translation was required had historically depended on the authority processing the application.

260 In order to avoid this confusion, the embassies and local immigration offices now have complete legal authority over the decision to issue a Blue Card and, in doing so, determining whether a degree is considered equivalent or not. A pre-approval from the employment office is now only seen as a recommendation and explicitly states that the embassy or immigration office must determine the equivalency of the degree in order to approve this permit type. This change leads to less disagreement between the authorities but can leave the applicant and company uncertain what to expect when applying if the university and degree type aren't both clearly listed.

How can one determine if a university degree is already recognized?

261 The online Database, ANABIN, lists degrees which have already been assessed for equivalency.[14] One can check online, sorting by country and degree types or subjects whether the university and the degree type is listed. A printout from the database of both these entries is considered sufficient proof of degree equivalency in Germany.

Both the university and degree type are listed in ANABIN, but they are not listed as being linked together. Do the university and degree type need to be linked in the database?

262 According to the department of foreign affairs, a university and a degree type do not need to be linked in the ANABIN database. As long as the entries are found separately, but linked to the country, this is sufficient (i.e. A B.A. or B.Sc. in Communications from a US institution is linked to the University of Illinois but not to the University of Iowa. This is, however, still considered a valid entry).

What if the university is listed but not the degree type?

263 If the university is listed but not the degree type, the application falls into a grey zone. While it is possible that the embassy still accepts the application as a Blue Card despite not having a full listing, there still remains a slight possibility that the local immigration office will notice this, be stricter in its assessment, and be unwilling to issue a Blue Card after arrival. In such a case, initiating a degree equivalency process would be the more secure way of proceeding.

14 ANABIN – http://anabin.kmk.org/anabin-datenbank.html (German only) – is an German acronym for "Anerkennung und Bewertung ausländischer Bildungsnachweise," roughly translated as, "Recognition and Evaluation of Foreign Education Certificates."

What if the degree is not already listed in the degree equivalency database?

If the degree is not listed or only partially listed, an official degree assessment to obtain a Statement of Comparability can be initiated. The Statement of Comparability confirms to the German authorities that the foreign degree is comparable to a German university degree. 264

Where can one obtain a Statement of Comparability?

The comparability assessment is performed by the Central Office for Foreign Education (ZAB – Zentralstelle für ausländisches Bildungswesen) at the Standing Conference of Education Ministers, the Federal Ministry for Economic Cooperation (KMK – Kultusministerkonferenz). 265

Who initiates the degree equivalency process?

The process is usually initiated by the person holding the degree. However, it can also be started by the company or third party assisting them. 266

What is the general process for obtaining a Statement of Comparability?

1. Check the website for the list of documents which need to be submitted according to the country of issuance of the foreign degree;
2. Register through the web-based form and receive the application form by e-mail;
3. Send the printed and signed form with the required documents to the ZAB by post;
4. Receives a notification of the fee to be paid once the documents arrive;
5. Transfer the fee (Note: checks are not accepted). As soon as the fee has been paid, the ZAB begins processing the application;
6. Submit any missing documents requested within 2 weeks of the request;
7. Issuing of the results of the comparability assessment by the examiner, who then mails the original to the applicant by post.

What documents are generally required?

The ANABIN website has a detailed tool to determine what documents need to be submitted for the equivalency process based on the country of issuance.[15] The website provides a list of countries and the required documents for each individual 267

---

15 https://www.kmk.org/kmk/information-in-english/statement-of-comparability-for-foreign-higher-education-qualifications/required-documentation.html.

country. Generally speaking, documents such as a certified copy of transcripts, a certified copy of the degree, proof of secondary school diploma allowing for university admittance, translations, a passport copy and a work contract (for Blue Card applications), etc. will need to be submitted. For a full list, the website should be visited.

How long does the process take?

268 The KMK states that processing times that Statements of Comparability for applying for a Blue Card should be issued within 2 weeks of the application if documents are complete and the payment is received within 7 working days. Experience has shown that processing times are approximately 3–4 weeks on average. The maximum processing time, according to the KMK, is 3 months.

269 It is to be noted, that the requirement to prove foreign degree equivalency to a German degree has increased drastically within the past months. This means that the volume of applications for assessment is on the rise and this could increase processing times.

How much does the process cost?

270 As of 2016, the costs are 200€ for the first statement, 100€ for any additional statements linked to an additional qualification, and 100€ for reissuance of a statement 20–100€ for cancellation or denial.

Is there anything else to be aware of?

271 The ANABIN database cannot list all universities and degrees worldwide, as the amount of data would be immense and the administrative effort overwhelming. It is therefore possible that some degrees have already been assessed but are not listed in the database.

If the examination result is negative and the degree is assessed as not recognized in Germany, can one take legal action against the decision?

272 Yes, one can lodge an appeal with the responsible authority and the case will be examined again. A complaint can be taken to the administrative court (Verwaltungsgericht). If the German judical process has been exhausted, the case can be brought to the European Court of Justice (Europäischen Gerichtshof).

6. Family Reunion

The nationality of the accompanying dependent and the principal applicant's nationality are the primary determinants for family reunion permits processes and requirements. 273

If the foreign dependent is an EU/EEA or Swiss national, they can enter Germany at any time (Please see chapter II. 2.2 – EU/EER[16] and Swiss nationals for further details). In these cases, the EU/EEA or Swiss National has a right to live and work in Germany, independent of the principal coming to Germany for employment purposes. 274

For non-EU/EEA or Swiss nationals the family reunion process and requirements are determined by the nationality of the principal, and broken down as follows: 275

- Family reunion to a German national (§28 AufenthG);
- Family reunion to an EU/EEA and Swiss national (§§2, 3, 4 FreizügG/EU);
- Family reunion to a non-EU/EEA or Swiss foreign national (§§29, 30, 32 AufenthG).

The residence permit for a foreign national will be granted for legally married spouses of a **German national**, minor children of German national and parents of a minor child holding German citizenship. 276

After arrival, spouses of German nationals usually receive a residence permit for the duration of three years at the first application. After that they are eligible to apply for permanent residence (Niederlassungserlaubnis). 277

Notably, dependents immigrating to Germany to join an **EU/EEA or Swiss national** have the right of freedom of movement if they are coming to live in Germany with the EU/EEA or Swiss national. 278

Upon arrival, the dependents immigrating to an EU/EEA or Swiss national receive a **residence permit for dependents of EU/EEA/Swiss Nationals** (Aufenthaltskarte), which is usually **valid for 5 years** at the first application. After that they can apply for permanent residence. 279

In general, the requirements for family reunion to a **foreign national in Germany** work in the following manner:[17] 280

- The foreign national living in Germany needs to have a permanent residence permit (Niederlassungserlaubnis), a permanent residence permit–EU (Daueraufenthalt-EU), a Blue Card EU, or a German residence permit (Aufenthaltserlaubnis);
- Sufficient housing space is available;

16 EER = European Economic Region.
17 This is in accordance with §29 AufenthG.

- The livelihood of the dependent coming to Germany is secured (including health insurance) without the usage of public funds;
- No grounds for expulsion (Ausweisungsgrund) exist.

281 Depending on the specific circumstances of each case, there may be other requirements that need to be fulfilled.

282 Dependents immigrating to a foreign (non-EU/EEA/Swiss) national receive a dependent's permit that is valid for the same duration as the principal applicant's permit.

283 Normally, the family reunion permit for spouses of both foreign and German nationals will only be issued if:
- both partners have reached the age of 18;
- the subsequently immigrating spouse has basic knowledge of the German language.

284 The process that dependents need to follow to enter Germany irrespective of the principal applicant's nationality mainly depends on their nationality. So, if the dependent is considered a non-visa national, there is no need to apply for an entry visa. However, if the dependent coming to Germany is a visa national, a visa application needs to be filed at the German mission in the home country.

285 Some exceptions apply such as for Brazilian nationals who are considered visa nationals, but, for the purpose of family reunion, they do not require an entry visa.[18]

Are their exemptions from the German language requirement?

286 Yes. The following exemptions, amongst others, apply for accompanying spouses and no knowledge of the German language needs to be proven for the issuance of either the entry visa or residence permit. This exemption applies when:
- The principal is an EU/EEA or Swiss national (except German nationals!);
- The principal holds a Blue Card EU;
- The principal works in Germany as a highly-qualified person, a researcher, or self-employed person and was already married when they moved to Germany;
- The spouse has recognizably minor need for integration (i.e. the spouse holds a university degree and it is expected that she/he will be able to find work in Germany on the basis of existing language skills);
- The spouse is incapable of demonstrating basic knowledge of the German language due to a physical or mental illness or handicap.

18 Please see chapter II. – Inbound for further clarification which nationalities are considered visa and non-visa nationals.

Who does not qualify for a dependent permit in Germany?

- Non-married partners (please see next question); 287
- Children over 18 years old;
- Parents/Grandparents/Other relatives;
- Au-Pair/nanny/domestic workers.

Are same sex couples legally recognized in Germany and can the partner join the principal?

Same sex marriage is recognized in Germany and the partner/spouse may join the 288
principal if they have a marriage certificate.

Are common law marriages recognized in Germany?

No. An official marriage certificate is required for the purpose of family reunion. 289

Can domestic workers be recognized as dependents and join employees coming on assignment?

Domestic workers are not recognized as dependents. However, there is a special 290
work permit category (§13 BeschV – Hausangestellte von Entsandten) based on which work permission may be given. This only applies to domestic workers of employees who are assigned to work in Germany, meaning that they are not coming on a local contract and are there for only for a limited time. For those domestic workers work permission can be granted if the domestic worker had worked for the employee assigned to work in Germany **at least one year before coming to Germany** and the purpose of his/her employment is taking care of a minor child under the age of 16 or another household member in need of care.

Will the family receive their entry visas at the same time as the principal will?

Most family reunion applications can be filed simultaneously with the principal, 291
however, family reunion visa processes can take a few weeks longer than the principal applicant. On average, family reunion visa processes can take 4–12 weeks.

Will spouses also receive the right to work in Germany?

Yes, a spouse will also automatically receive the right to work in Germany without 292
any additional paperwork required.

7. Legalization/Apostille

293 Some documents require authentication as proof that they are real in the form of a **legalization** or **apostille** in order for them to be recognized by a country as a legally valid document. Which form of **authentication** is required mainly depends on the country where the document is going to be used. Legalization involves obtaining a final stamp on the document from a consular officer of the embassy or consulate of the destination country (country where the document will be used). The apostille is a simplified form of obtaining document authentication for which certain countries have signed a treaty[19].

294 The Hague Convention of 5 October 1961 Abolishing the Requirement of Legalization for Foreign Public Documents is a treaty that removes the requirement to obtain full legalization by an embassy or consulate on foreign public documents. The countries that have signed this treaty have a reciprocal agreement that documents requiring authentication no longer need to include the final stamp from the embassy or consulate abroad. This means that the document exchange between two countries that are part of The Hague Convention benefit from a simplified, shortened process[20].

Foreign documents for use in Germany

295 In order to be accepted at certain German authorities, some documents must be legalized or apostilled. These documents would typically be submitted at various stages of the immigration process. This is most commonly done when requesting the point of entry visa, at address registration (less common), or for the residence permit application at the immigration office (quite common). This requirement varies between the different German authorities and jurisdictions and may also vary depending on the country of origin of the certificate/document. Legalized or apostilled documents may also be requested at the discretion of the authorities responsible for reviewing the documents. Proper research of document requirements at the different authorities involved is a very important part of the processes needed to avoid unpleasant surprises and potential delays.

296 Once the requirement is determined, the applicant must research what steps need to be performed in the document's country of origin in order to collect the re-

19 For a full list of the countries who have signed the treaty of the Hague Convention of 5 October 1961 Abolishing the Requirement of Legalization for Foreign Public Documents please see: https://www.hcch.net/en/instruments/conventions/status-table/?cid=41.

20 For an English-language site with more information about the apostille process, see: http://www.auswaertigesamt.de/EN/Laenderinformationen/01Laender/Konsularisches/UrkundenverkehrTeilA_node.html.

quired legalization or apostille stamp. The process can involve several steps at different offices (such as civil registry offices, the department of foreign affairs [State Department in the USA], embassy, etc.) and can take several weeks – or even months – depending on the country and complexity of the process.

Documents that are commonly required to have a legalization or apostille for the immigration process in Germany are marriage certificates (for accompanying spouses), birth certificates (for accompanying children), and sometimes university degree certificates (for the main applicant). It is not usually necessary to have other documents legalized for the standard immigration process to Germany, however, the immigration authorities reserve the right to request this at any time. **297**

German documents for use abroad

The same requirement for the handling of foreign documents can be made for German documents for their use abroad. **298**

The most common German documents requiring legalization or apostille for the immigration process for use abroad are marriage certificates, birth certificates, university degrees, police clearance certificates, and employment confirmation letters. **299**

Each document type has different authorities which need to be involved in the process. **300**

For marriage and birth certificates, the process usually begins with the issuance of a new excerpt from the civil registry/bureau of vital statistics (Standesamt), as this type of certificate can only be legalized if it was issued 6 months or less prior. The district or regional council (Bezirksregierung/Regierungspräsidium) responsible in the German state (Bundesland) where the document originates must then certify the certificate either directly with the apostille or a pre-legalization. This process is performed so that it can then be presented to the embassy or consulate of the destination country for legalization. **301**

The university degree certification process often starts by obtaining a certified copy of the degree issued by the university, followed by the district or regional council and where required, the embassy or consulate of the destination country. **302**

For purposes of legalization/apostille and use in another country, a German police clearance certificate (polizeiliches Führungszeugnis) may not be older than 3 months and pre-legalization or the apostille process is carried out by the Federal Office of Administration (Bundesverwaltungsamt). **303**

Employment confirmation letters can be signed in front of a notary and afterwards receive the apostille or pre-legalization stamp at the **regional court** (Landgericht) where the notary is registered. **304**

The regional court is also responsible for the authentication of translations as all registered translators are listed there. **305**

It is insufficient to have a simple copy or, in some cases, an older version of a certificate for authentication. To be eligible for legalization or apostille, the docu- **306** ment in question must be newly issued or be certified with the original signature of an officer or representative who is recognized by the authorized office that will issue the legalization stamp or apostille. Each authorized office will have a signature sample of the recognized signatories on file.

307 As each document must go through a number of steps that may need to be performed in several different cities with varying processing times. Thus, the process can be long. Some steps can be concluded in person, others need to be filed by post. It is therefore essential to allow **at least 2 months** for processing, as one may need several weeks before the final document is legalized/apostilled.

What countries have signed The Hague Convention and the apostille process that can be followed?

308 For a full list of countries who have signed The Hague Convention, please see https://www.hcch.net/en/instruments/conventions/status-table/?cid=41.

Can a country still sign The Hague Convention at a later date and become an "apostille country"?

309 Yes. Countries are still able to sign the treaty and become eligible for the simplified apostille process.

If only one of the two countries involved have signed The Hague Convention, can an apostille still be issued?

310 If only one country involved has signed the treaty (e.g. Germany) but the other has not (e.g. Canada), the apostille will not be an accepted form of authentication and a legalization will need to be obtained.

What documents can be legalized/apostilled?

311 Only public certificates issued from government bodies (e.g. civil registry, governmental universities, the Federal Department of Justice) can be legalized. A notary must certify private documents – such as company letters – before they are recognized as public.

What documents cannot be legalized/apostilled?

312 It is sometimes very tricky or impossible to obtain authentication for degrees issued by private universities.

Are there countries whose documents cannot be legalized for use in Germany?

The German authorities have experienced in the past that, in some countries, the forgery of documents is commonplace, and the legalization process cannot be considered trustworthy. In these countries (e.g. India), a special verification process for documents has been implemented. This involves an external support for verifying if, for example, a marriage certificate is authentic by means of viewing photos and videos of the wedding, all the way to personal home visits to speak to neighbors and relatives about the couple in question. This process can take up to 12 weeks. 313

Are any countries or documents exempted from the legalization/apostille requirement?

Some countries (e.g. Austria) have a bilateral agreement with Germany that allows for the acceptance of all documents as long as they have been stamped by the official authority in that country. 314

Does the legalization need to be placed on an original document or can it be on a certified copy?

This depends on the type of document and the country of origin. For example, German birth and marriage certificates must always be originals in order for them to be legalized. Some countries may only accept a legalized university degree on the original, whereas others may accept a certified copy. 315

What is a certified copy?

A certified copy is a photocopy of an original document made by an official representative. The individuals who are allowed to issue certified copies can vary from country to country, however it is often a notary, an embassy, a town hall, or sometimes even the church. 316

Is there a standardized form of stamp for the legalization?

No. Each embassy will have their own format for issuing the legalization stamp. 317

Is there a standardized form of stamp for the apostille?

Yes. The apostille stamp has a standardized, recognizable structure always with the word APOSTILLE at the top and with ten set fields with information on issuing country, name of official signatory, number of the apostille, date etc. to be completed with relevant the information. 318

Are translations of the documents required? Is it part of the process?

319 Some but not all countries have translation integrated into the legalization/apostille process. Often the translation is the final step of the process.

What are the fees for legalization/apostille in Germany?

320 Government fees vary per document and per step. For example, new civil status certificates currently usually cost around 10–12€, pre-legalization or apostille 15–35€, and the legalization at the embassy is dependent on the individual embassy's fees for this service.

8. Red Flags

321 There are certain things to keep an eye out for during all stages of the immigration process, as these can create obstacles that may delay the intended start date of the assignment or employment, or even make securing a German work permit impossible. In addition, family reunion processes can take longer than the primary applicant. This may cause further delays, especially in cases where the primary applicant does not want to travel without his or her family.

322 With this in view, here is a collection of red flags for which applicants should watch.

Which red flags are there to watch out for during the work permit process?

323
- *Lack of university degree* – several work permit categories require the applicant to have a university level education. In some cases, several years of work experience can replace a university degree. However, in other cases, such as with the Blue Card EU permit, a recognized degree is necessary.
- *University degree not listed in the German equivalency database (ANABIN) or listed as "limitedly comparable"* – In some cases, simply having a university degree is insufficient. The degree needs to be listed in the ANABIN database for purpose of recognition in Germany. For more details on the recognition process please see chapter 5.
- *Degree type does not logically match the job to be performed* (i.e. Mathematician in a marketing position). Unless the company can convincingly prove the importance of the applicant for this position, the application cannot be approved.
- *Position lower in the hierarchy or educational qualification not required for position* – The German employment office reserves the right to reject an application based on the strong assumption that there are unemployed German or other EU nationals already living in Germany who possess the skills required to fill and

subsequently perform these positions for lower level positions, such as positions not requiring:
- a degree;
- specific vocational training.

Examples of these include secretarial and other assistant positions. 324
- *Assignee has not worked for employer outside Germany for more than 12 months yet* – for the most common work permit for assignees on secondment (§29 (5) BeschV – International Agreement), the law text dictates that the assignee must work for at least 12 months for the company outside Germany in order to be eligible.
- *Salary too low* – Although Germany does not publish a chart of minimum salary ranges for employing foreigners in Germany, it does have a regulation stating that a foreigner may not be paid less than a German working in the same job with similar qualifications. For example, an Indian national on assignment to Germany cannot continue to be paid his base salary only, as this would present conditions less favorable than a German in the same position. As a rule of thumb, currently anything above approx. 3000€ gross per month for any type of qualified employment is usually accepted.
- *Allowances that are not paid out as a lump sum* – Allowances paid to the employee to cover costs such as accommodation or transport which help reach the minimum salary requirement must be paid out as a lump sum for the employee to use as he/she wishes and not be paid out only upon receipt. Rent must not be paid directly by the company but by the employee using his own allowances.

Which red flags should an applicant be aware of during the residence permit process?

- *Address registration using a hotel address* – Before filing for the residence permit, the employee needs to register his local address. In order to do so he or she needs to submit a written address confirmation to the registration office that has been signed by his or her landlord. Many hotels will not issue a landlord confirmation for stays under 2 months, which sometimes makes registration in a temporary hotel accommodation tricky. 325
- *Non-visa nationals must pay particular attention to securing long-term accommodation on time* – Non-visa nationals who complete all their immigration steps after arrival need to take care to secure long-term accommodation at an address with which they can register immediately after arrival in Germany. This step is mandatory for securing the residence permit needed to allow the commencement of work in Germany. As such, any delay in registering with a long-term accommodation address can lead to a delay in the ability to begin working.

- *Non-visa nationals who have almost exhausted their Schengen days allowance prior to employment begin* – Using up too many of the 90 allowed Schengen days on business before applying for a work/residence permit can be problematic. In order to be able to return once the 90 days are almost used up, a non-visa national may need to revert to obtaining an entry visa from the consulate – before re-entry – to finish the immigration process.
- *Insufficient proof of expat health insurance for assignees* – Some jurisdictions have strict requirements for health insurance proof for assignees – i.e. Hamburg, Maintaunus Kreis (in the Greater Frankfurt am Main area), etc. – and will not issue the final residence permit until sufficient health insurance is in place.
- *Re-registration from one jurisdiction to another in the middle of the immigration process* – changing jurisdictions before the residence permit process is complete may disrupt the process and cause delays. The process generally follows these steps:
  - The city registration office will inform the immigration office of anyone who has recently moved into that jurisdiction.
  - The immigration file then gets sent from one jurisdiction to the immigration office in the new jurisdiction.
  - It can take 3–6 weeks for file transfer to be complete, causing delays while it is in transit.

Which red flags should an applicant be aware of in regards to travel?

326 – *Non-visa nationals who have exceeded the 90 day Schengen allowance* – If a non-visa national has received a temporary permit so they can stay in Germany while the final permit is being processed but have already exceeded the 90-day Schengen business allowance before the final residence permit is issued, the temporary permit will not allow them to travel and they will need to stay in Germany until the process is complete.
- *Non-visa nationals entering into the Schengen area through other country than the final destination (Germany)* – This may cause questioning by the border control of the Schengen country of entry, especially if the stay is not Schengen business but for working purposes with a final destination of Germany.

Which red flags are there to watch out for in regards to family members/family reunion?

327 – *Unmarried partners* – "common law marriage" is not recognized in Germany. A couple must be married in order for the partner to qualify as a dependant.
- Adopted children or split custody – This situation can cause delays in visa processing. Additional documentation and permission may be necessary.

- Child moving to Germany with only one parent – In the case of split custody, additional approval will be required by the parent not travelling to Germany.
- Language requirement for spouses before being able to receive entry visa – In some cases, the embassy may insist that the accompanying spouse have at least A1 German language skills before they will issue the entry visa for Germany.
- Language requirement for accompanying children who arrive in Germany after their 16th birthday – The German authorities can request that the child obtain C1 German language knowledge before issuing him/her a long-term residence permit.
- Language requirement for spouses of a German national – While spouses of EU nationals other than Germans are exempt from any language requirement, spouses of German nationals need to prove at least A1 German language skills to obtain a residence permit.
- Marriage took place **after** the primary applicant has moved to Germany – In this case couple may be required to wait for 2 years before a family reunion can take place.
- Legalization of marriage and birth certificates – The legalization or apostille process can take several weeks. In certain countries, like India and the Philippines, it is an extremely long process, potentially delaying any family reunion for up to 4 months.
- Assignments under 12 months duration – Some jurisdictions will not approve family reunion for duration less than 12 months.

9. Non-compliance – Penalties and monetary fines

Non-compliance with German immigration rules is taken very seriously, and there **328**
is a threat of severe legal consequences for those who violate law related to them. German authorities are often very strict when immigration law violations are discovered, and there are numerous consequences for both the employee and employer alike.

A breach of German immigration law can be, for example, illegal employment **329**
that includes working without a work permit or even working with an incorrect permit type. An example of working with the wrong permit type would include carrying out work based on the incorrect legal basis or limitation to a certain profession or region.

Probably the most common breach of German immigration law happens when **330**
employees travel to Germany to perform work activities while on a business traveler status only. This violation is rarely discovered through random company audits but may be detected through questioning at the border when entering.

Another common breach includes cases where a visa waiver national (nationals **331**
permitted to travel to the Schengen area for business and tourist purposes with their

passport only) overstays and exceeds the allowed 90 days within a 180-day period on this status. Discovery of such a violation often results an obligation to leave (Ausreisepflicht), a monetary fine (Geldstrafe bzw. Bußgeld oder Freiheitsstrafe), or a travel ban (Reiseverbot). In cases where the allowed 90 days are only exceeded by a few days, the immigration authority may make an exception and let the traveler leave without having to pay a fine or initiate an official legal procedure against that traveler.

332 The level of penalty for both the employee and the employer depends on severity of the violation.

333 For the employee the consequences can be:
- Monetary fine or imprisonment;
- Obligation to leave;
- Expulsion (Ausweisung);
- Deportation/Arrest (Abschiebung/Festnahme);
- Restrictions in re-entering the country (e.g. travel ban).

334 Employers need to ensure compliance with German immigration rules, since having foreign employees without the required German work and residence permit work in Germany is considered a criminal or administrative offence (Straftat oder Ordnungswidrigkeit).

335 The consequences of a breach of German immigration law for employers can be:
- Liability for costs of deportation;
- Monetary fine up to 500,000 EUR (§404 SGB[21] III) for illegal employment of foreign nationals.

336 The authority could refuse subsequent work permit applications for employees coming to Germany, if, within the last five years, the employing company:
- has had to pay a monetary fine according to §§404 (1) or (2) No 5 SGB III;
- was convicted based on violations against the Control of Unreported Employment Act (Schwarzarbeitsbekämpfungsgesetz – SchwarzArbG) or Temporary Employment Act (Arbeitnehmerüberlassungsgesetz – AÜG);
- Exclusion from public procurement procedures and from obtaining subsidies.

337 While the above consequences are the legal consequences of a non-compliance situation, the massive negative impact on the company's public face, its reputation, is a matter of utmost importance for those wanting to do business in Germany. Once a company has been in the public view with reports of German immigration law vio-

21 SGB is the abbreviation for the German Social Security Act.

lations, this leaves a negative impression on clients, authorities and the general public, which, logically, will end up impacting the company bottom line.

Where is a travel ban registered?

Any travel ban is noted in the Central register of foreigners (Ausländerzentralregister). This can be accessed by border control police and German embassies/consulates. 338

Can employees lodge an appeal against the decisions of a penalty?

Yes. The usual appeal processes against monetary and administrative fines apply for violations against immigration law. 339

Is there usually a distinction in penalty made based on the type of traveler (non-visa or visa national)?

No. The same penalties apply, regardless of the nationality. 340

III. Outbound

1 As detailed throughout this book, many foreigners are coming to Germany for employment purposes. On the other hand, more and more companies are also sending their employees on assignment from Germany to various international destinations. In the context of increasing globalization, it has become increasingly important for companies operating internationally to place their employees all over the world. International assignments are mainly for the benefit of the company, with benefits ranging from production line improvements, to standardization of international processes and to global knowledge transfer through exchange of personnel. In most cases, these "expat" assignments end up benefitting the assigned employee as much as they do the company. Through an assignment abroad, employees have a direct international exchange of experiences with co-workers all over the world, including the opportunity to increase their knowledge of a foreign culture, including languages. There is no doubt that such intercultural exchanges of experiences make the day-to-day operations in an company functioning internationally easier through raised awareness and acceptance.

2 When planning international assignments from Germany to any destination, many factors have to be taken into account. Amongst others, employment law matters, the personal tax situation as well as the social security situation of each employee play an important role and need to be considered carefully. In this chapter, we will take a closer look at the immigration implications of an assignment from Germany.

3 Each destination country has to be looked at individually, as there is no "one" immigration process that applies to all countries. It is fair to say that assignments within the EU/EEA usually do not require an extensive immigration process for other EU/EEA nationals. Freedom of movement rights are based on European Law and were therefore implemented in all EU member states. The only thing to watch out for is concerning registration obligations. Each EU/EEA country has its own regulations on how an individual has to register there. Though Germany only requires an EU/EEA national to register his or her address (same process applies for any German national), other EU/EEA countries have stricter regulations on registration of foreign workers.

4 In case of an assignment into non EU/EEA nation, each case has to be assessed individually. The following points in almost all cases play a role in assessing the immigration process for a given expat.

Nationality of the individual

5 Even though, in most cases, the nationality of foreign assignment applicants sent from Germany carry a German passport, it is worth double checking for a few reasons, such as:

- the assignee could have a dual nationality that allows him or her either easier access to the respective destination country (e.g. citizens of the countries that are members of the EAEU[22]) do not require a work permit in Russia);
- a second nationality could make the immigration process more difficult (e.g. Israeli passport holders are restricted from entry into UAE).

Immigration status in Germany

If the individual is not a German or EU/EEA national, prior to the assignment, the 6
immigration status of the individual needs to be looked at very carefully. In some cases the German immigration status can have an impact on the process that needs to be followed in the host country. More importantly, what impact the absence from Germany can have on the immigration status needs to be considered. In general, German residence permits (even permanent residency permits) lose their validity if the individual has left Germany for more than six months. For Blue Card EU cardholders, this timeframe is extended to 12 months. Should the company send the employee back to Germany after an assignment abroad, the immigration office in Germany responsible should be contacted before the employee leaves Germany in order to apply for and collect a notification of return. This allows the individual to remain outside of Germany for longer than 6 months, or 12 months for holders of the Blue Card EU. The application can be filed for if the company is willing to confirm in writing that they plan to send the employee back to Germany. Particularly for future German permanent residency applications, German citizenship applications, or both, it is important to have this official confirmation from the immigration office. Both German permanent residency and citizenship applications require the individual to be considered a legal resident of Germany for a certain amount of years. Only when the immigration office is informed and confirms in writing that the deadline has been extended can the time spent outside of Germany continue to count towards the collective years needed in order to file these kinds of applications. Without this confirmation, the time accrued up until departure would no longer be taken into account, and the applicant would need to start accruing the years necessary for satisfying the application requirements once they return from abroad.

Planned duration of stay in destination country

Some countries have special permit types for short-term assignments or even allow 7
working without a work permit for a limited duration of stay.

---

22 Eurasian Economic Union (EAEU) currently includes five nations: Armenia, Belarus, Kazakhstan and Kyrgyzstan, and The Russian Federation.

Description of tasks to be performed in destination country

8 A detailed description of the tasks that are going to be performed in the destination country is essential for the classification of the travel: Can the tasks be performed on a business traveler status or is a full work permit required? While some countries define business travel rather strictly, (only attend meetings, no production work) other countries allow certain work activities (e.g. installation or assembly work) on a business visitor status.

9 We have taken a few common destination countries to highlight some of the differences and similarities in immigration processes across the globe: USA, UAE, China, Switzerland, Singapore, Russia, Brazil. The following chapters, you will gain see the answer to some key questions about the processes in the selected countries, including:

- What is the government's policy towards corporate immigration?
- What is the general process and processing time?
- What are the most common permit types?
- What are the red flags to watch out for?

1. USA

What is the U.S.A's policy towards corporate immigration?

10 The US government's policy towards corporate immigration is one that attempts to strike a balance between labor market protectionism and the free flow of foreign individuals into the US workforce. As such, much of US immigration law consists of rules and procedures that in many instances facilitate, and in other instances impede, the admission of foreign individuals to the United States for business purposes.

11 Despite the conflicting values underlying the United States' immigration regulations, the current US immigration system, on a broad level, does in fact have a coherent policy towards corporate immigration. First, as a matter of policy, individuals who are seeking entry to the US for business purposes that will not result in the traveler entering the US labor market are eligible for admission to the US for a relatively short period of stay. Second, foreign individuals seeking admission to the US for the purpose of entering the US labor market must meet the requirements of a particular work visa category, which, depending on one's qualifications and prospective work arrangement in the US, can be quite restrictive.

What is the general process and processing times?

12 Individuals seeking admission to the US for business purposes, but who will not be entering the US labor market, are classified as B-1 business visitors. Those who are seeking entry to the US to work are classified as workers.

The process for obtaining admission to the US, and the processing time, depends on whether or not the individual seeking entry to the US is a business visitor or worker, as well as many other factors. Below is a general overview of the process and approximate processing times for those seeking admission to the US as a business visitor and those seeking admission to the US as a worker: 13

1.1 Business Visitors

Canadian Citizens

Process

Canadians are not required to obtain a visa to enter the US as a business visitor. Instead, Canadians are permitted entry into the US, provided the US immigration officer at the airport or border concludes that the traveler is a bona fide business visitor. 14

Processing Time

Admission is granted immediately at the airport or border. 15

Citizens of a Visa Waiver Program Country

Process

The visa waiver program is a US program that allows citizens of certain countries who are seeking entry into the US as a tourist or business visitor to enter the United States for up to 90 days without having to obtain a visa. 16

To enter the US as a business visitor without having to obtain a visa, citizens of visa waiver countries must first register with an automated government system before travelling. The system is referred to as the Electronic System for Travel Authorization ("ESTA").[23] 17

Citizens of visa waiver countries who are registered with ESTA will be granted admission to the US, provided the US immigration officer at the border or airport concludes that the traveler is a bona fide business visitor. 18

Processing Time

Admission is granted immediately at the airport or border. 19

23 See https://travel.state.gov/content/visas/en/visit/visa-waiver-program.html for more details.

Citizens of Other Countries

Process

20 Those who do not hold Canadian citizenship, and individuals who are not citizens of a visa waiver country, will not be admitted to the US as a business visitor unless they are in possession of a B-1 visa.

21 To obtain a B-1 visa, one must submit an online form and schedule a visa appointment at a US Consulate or Embassy. If the visa application is approved, the visa will be issued. Once the traveler is in receipt of the visa, he or she may seek admission into the US by presenting the visa to the US immigration officer at the airport or border.

Processing Time

22 The processing time for the B-1 visa application process depends on the wait time for the US Consulate or Embassy where the applicant will attend his or her appointment. The processing time also depends on the amount of time it takes for the Consulate or Embassy to issue the visa after the appointment. The total application processing time, depending on the Consulate or Embassy where the applicant will attend his or her appointment, can range anywhere from a few days to several months.

1.2 Workers

Port-of-Entry Applications

Process

23 For certain work visa categories, Canadians can submit their application at a designated port-of-entry (authorized border crossings and airports) while on route to the US. A US immigration officer at the port-of-entry will adjudicate the application on the spot.

Processing

24 If the application is approved, the applicant's work authorization status will be issued on the spot.

Consulate Applications

Process

25 For certain work visa categories, one must schedule a visa appointment and submit their visa application at a US Consulate or Embassy. If the application is approved, the Consulate or Embassy will issue the work visa after the appointment.

Processing Time

The processing time for a Consular-based work visa application depends on the wait time for the US Consulate or Embassy where the applicant has his or her appointment and the amount of time it takes for the Consulate or Embassy to issue the work visa after the appointment. The total application processing time, depending on the Consulate or Embassy where the applicant has his or her appointment, can range anywhere from a couple weeks to several months. 26

Non-immigrant Petitions

Process

In US immigration parlance, a non-immigrant is an individual who intends on entering the US for a temporary period as opposed to entering the US with the intent of residing in the US permanently. As such, a non-immigrant petition is a petition filed for the benefit of an individual who intends on working, and possibly living, in the US for a temporary period. The petition is filed with, and adjudicated by, the United States Citizenship and Immigration Services (USCIS). 27

For certain work visa categories, a petitioner (typically a US employer) must file a non-immigrant petition for the benefit of the foreign individual who is seeking to work in the United States for the US employer. If the petition is approved, the applicant will need to submit a visa application and schedule a visa appointment at a US Consulate or Embassy. If the visa application is approved, the Consulate or Embassy will issue the work visa after the appointment. 28

Processing Time

The entire application process, including the processing time for the USCIS adjudication of the petition, and the Consulate, or Embassy, visa processing time, can range anywhere from several weeks to several months. 29

What are the most common permit types?

The two most common types of work visa categories are the L-1 intracompany transferee visa and the H-1B specialty occupation work visa. The purpose and eligibility requirements for these two work visa categories are as follows: 30

1.3 L-1 Intracompany Transferee Visa

The L-1 is a work visa category that allows employees to transfer to an office or legal entity in the US that has a specific corporate relationship with the employee's employer abroad. 31

32 For one to be eligible for an L-1, the following requirements must be met:

1. **Qualifying Relationship:** The U.S. office where the employee will be transferred must be a branch office, parent, subsidiary, affiliate or joint venture partner of the employer abroad.
2. **One Year of Employment:** The transferee must have been employed by the foreign employer as an executive, manager or in a specialized knowledge capacity for at least one year, without interruption, within the last three years.
3. **Position with the US Company:** The transferee must be entering the US to work in an executive, managerial or specialized knowledge position.

1.4 H-1B Specialty Occupation Visa

33 An H-1B is a work visa category for individuals who will work in a specialty occupation while in the US. A specialty occupation is one that requires (a) a theoretical and practical application of a body of specialized knowledge, and (b) the attainment of a bachelor's degree (or higher) in the specific specialty (or its equivalent) as a minimum for entry into the occupation in the United States.

34 For one to be eligible for an H-1B, the following requirements must be met, wherein the applicant must:

- have the equivalent of a US Bachelor's degree, or the equivalent, in education and/or work experience;
- be offered a job to work in a position that requires a US Bachelor's degree or the equivalent;
- be placed on the US company's payroll once they commence employment with the US employer; and
- be paid the prevailing wage while working for the US employer (the prevailing wage is defined as the average wage paid to similarly employed workers in a specific occupation in the area of intended employment).

What are some typical red flags to watch out for?

35 The following is a four-step process to increase the likelihood of successful business travel to the US:

36 Consult with a US immigration attorney to determine whether the purpose of entry to the US constitutes permissible business visitor activity or necessitates a work visa.

- If a grey area, err on the side of caution and have the employee obtain a work visa.

37 If the employee will be engaging in work, identify the most appropriate work visa.

- The H-1B visa and the L-1 visa are the two most common work visas, but other types of visas may be more appropriate.
  If necessary, have the employee obtain the appropriate work visa.
- This includes ensuring that the application/petition is properly prepared, all necessary supporting documents are provided, and all relevant procedure is followed (a US immigration attorney should be retained to handle this process).

2. United Arab Emirates

What is the UAE's policy towards corporate immigration?

Policies relating to the employment of United Arab Emirates (UAE) and foreign na- **38**
tionals are maintained by the Federal Ministry of Human Resources and Emiratization 'MOHRE' (formerly the Ministry of Labor and Social Affairs), and, generally speaking, labor laws in the UAE is loosely based on the International Labor Organization's model. In 2003, the UAE launched an initiative aimed towards increasing the participation of national employees in the workforce. This policy of 'Emiratization' aims to employ citizens in a meaningful and efficient manner in the public and private sectors, as this contributes to a successful economic and political structure. Emiratization works through the implementation of prescribed percentages in certain business sectors as well as requiring certain positions to be fulfilled by UAE nationals. However, despite the underlying framework for Emiratization, there remains a heavy reliance on expatriate workers, and Emiratization policies are not strictly enforced in certain sectors and geographical locations.

To the latter point, the UAE also maintains several geographically distinct areas **39**
referred to as 'Freezones'. Freezones allow 100% foreign ownership and, from an immigration perspective, do not fall under the direct purview of the MOHRE. Freezones operate their own Government Services Offices (GSOs) that liaise with the immigration authorities on behalf of the sponsoring entity and also tend follow a relatively streamlined work authorization process. However, documentation requirements (and subsequent processing times) tend to vary from Freezone to Freezone.

What is the general process and processing times?

The process is determined based on whether the company is based onshore or off- **40**
shore.

2.1 Onshore companies

41 The employer must:

1. Apply and obtain approval for a quota of employment with the MOHRE.
   NOTE: This step will not apply if a quota has already been granted previously. If previously granted, the process will start from step 2 below.
2. Prepare an offer letter from the MOHRE. Both employee and the employer are required to sign that letter.
3. Once approval of the employment from the MOHRE has been obtained, pay the visa application fees and deposit a bank guarantee amount.
4. Submit the employment entry permit application and supporting documents to the immigration authorities in the UAE.
5. When the application is approved and an employment entry permit is granted, the employee can then enter the UAE, undergo a medical examination and submit their biometric information so that an Emirates ID card can be issued.
6. Acquire a government-approved healthcare insurance plan for the employee.
7. Once the medical results have been received by the employer, prepare, sign and submit the local labor contract to the MOHRE for approval.
8. Once the MOHRE approves the contract, submit the employment residence permit (ERP) stamping application and required supporting documents to the immigration authorities for approval.

2.2 Offshore companies

42 The Freezone company will be required to undertake steps 4 to 8 listed above, with the exception of step 7, which does not need to be completed. Applications are made to the Government Services Office of the relevant Freezone rather than the MOHRE.

2.3 Processing timelines

43 The process of obtaining a work permit and initial visa takes approximately four to five weeks depending on the jurisdiction where the entity is established. If the application is subject to a security screening, the standard processing times will not apply.

What are the most common permit types?

1. Mission Work Permit:

44 A Mission Work Permit is a temporary work permit issued to foreign nationals. This work permit is a non-extendable, single-entry permit valid for a period of 90 days. The

permit allows the individual to work. Such visas are granted and issued subject to approval from the MOHRE. Mission work permits allow the holder to engage in hands-on/technical work and are usually meant to facilitate short-term contractual obligations in relation to a project. Please note that mission entry permits cannot be converted into employment visas and holders need to exit the country prior to expiry.

Mission Work Permit applications require MOHRE employment contracts in place for short-term work. 45

2. Employment Residence Permit (ERP):

The main immigration category used by the employer to hire foreign nationals is an employment residence permit. ERPs are valid for two years for onshore companies and three years for offshore companies. They permit multiple entry and can be renewed upon expiry. 46

Requirements:

Each permit or visa has its own requirements and procedures. However, certain general conditions must be satisfied in most instances. Here is a useful listing of those conditions: 47

1. Employee specific requirements:
   - the applicant must hold a passport that has a remaining validity of at least six months at the time of application. However, it is recommended a **minimum validity** period of **six months** at **all stages** of the process;
   - the relevant authorities (GDRFA or MOHRE) have approved the applicant's visa/permit application;
   - the applicant should not be banned from entering the UAE (prior Labor or immigration ban) and does not belong to any of the nationalities or categories disallowed by the UAE immigration authorities on the grounds of national security, domestic policy, or both;
   - the applicant is free from communicable diseases – certain visa/permit categories require the applicant to complete an in-country medical examination;
   - the applicant has valid academic credentials that can be presented as part of the work authorization application (certain managerial/professional job titles would require this).
2. Employer specific requirements:
   - the sponsoring entity must be in good standing with the MOHRE, GDRFA, as well as the relevant Freezone authority (if applicable);
   - the sponsoring entity must have all valid, up-to-date corporate and corporate immigration documentation and must be licensed to conduct business in its relevant jurisdiction;

- the sponsoring entity must have the relevant quotas and sponsorship permissions in place (if applicable).

What are the 5–7 typical red flags to watch out for?

48 1. Israeli passport holders are restricted from entry into the UAE, and their immigration applications are therefore likely to result in a negative outcome.
2. Immigration applications from Iranian and Iraqi passport holders undergo stringent security screening and obtaining positive outcome of their applications is very difficult.
3. Individuals from the below countries undergo additional security checks and will be required to provide additional documents for processing of their immigration permits in the UAE:
   - Afghanistan
   - Arab nationals with European passports
   - Libya
   - Somalia
   - South Africa
   - Sri Lanka
   - Syria
4. The MOHRE may impose an automatic labor ban on individuals who have worked for their current employer in the UAE for under six months and will require additional supporting documents for their immigration applications.
5. Applications from a female main applicant sponsoring her spouse are reviewed on a case-to-case basis and they are required to earn more than male main applicants.
6. Unmarried and same sex partners are not recognized as dependents in the UAE and will need to obtain residence status in their own right.

3. China

What is China's policy towards corporate immigration?

49 Corporate immigration in China is jointly governed by the Ministry of Human Resources and Social Security ("MHRSS"), Ministry of Foreign Affairs, and Ministry of Public Security.

50 All foreign nationals (including residents from Hong Kong, Macau and Taiwan) must obtain an Employment Permit in order to work in China.

51 There are two documents for which business expats wishing to work in China need to apply for and obtain:

- Single-entry Z Visa, which is for initial first entry into China and is valid for only 30 days);
- Resident Permit (to be applied within 30 days after arriving China).

Residents from Hong Kong, Macau and Taiwan are not subjected to this visa requirement and are able to travel and reside in China as holders of the Home Return Pass. 52

What is the general process and processing times?

Employment permit is city specific, and the applicant is required to work in the same location as the sponsoring company. 53

The key stages in the application process to obtain the work visa in China are: 54

1. Application by the employer for an Employment License (if the employee will be working for a Foreign Investment Enterprise) or Working Card (for a Foreign Representative Office).
2. Invitation Letter issued by the local commercial bureau and addressed to the relevant Chinese Embassy or Consulate.
3. Application for a (single-entry) Z visa prior to entering China.
4. Medical Examination
   In order to be considered eligible for obtaining an Employment Permit, the foreign national must undergo a medical examination at an authorized hospital.
5. Employment Permit
   The applicant must apply for an Employment Permit within 30 days of arrival in China, following successful completion of a medical examination.
6. Application for Foreigner Residence Permit
   Once an Employment Permit has been granted, the applicant must then apply for a Foreigner Residence Permit, which must also be applied for within 30 days of arrival in China. Therefore, stages five and six must be completed within the same time frame.

Although the application process is similar national-wide, the local practice may vary from city to city. For example, Beijing has implemented a new online system effective 4 January 2016 for processing applications for employment licenses, employment permits and expert permits submitted by local entities for their employing of foreign individuals. On-site submission can only be arranged after the online approval has been obtained. 55

The processing time for completion of all stages for a standard application is approximately ten weeks. This may vary depending on the supporting documents required by the relevant authority. 56

For Beijing, due to the additional online pre-approval process, it will take another two to four weeks in aggregate for application of employment license and employment permit or expert permit. 57

What are the most common permit types?

58 Employment Permit is the most commonly seen permit type for foreign individuals working in China for over 90 days.

59 In assessing an application, the authorities will consider factors including whether:

- the applicant is employed by an establishment of a foreign company in China;
- the applicant possesses adequate competencies, including work experience and academic credentials required for the post in China;
- the position can easily be filled by a local individual.

60 Supporting documents usually include a resume, academic and professional qualification certificates, Employment License or Working Card and Invitation Letter. Documents must be in Chinese and display the local entity's company stamp.

61 As a reminder, the consular officer may require the applicant to provide other documents or supplementary materials, or require an interview with the applicant.

62 Following the Employment Permit's issuance, a Residence Permit (also known as the Z work visa) needs to be applied for so that the applicant to reside in China. The Residence Permit usually has the same validity period as the Employment Permit.

M Visa	F Visa
providing machinery and equipment maintenance, installation, testing, debugging, disassembling, inspection and training providing guidance, supervision and inspection on successful bids working short-term in branches, subsidiaries and representative offices, and participating in athletic competitions (including athletes, coaches, doctors and assistants unless otherwise approved by the in-charge authorities as requested by the international athletic associations).	performing volunteer work either receiving no pay or receiving pay from overseas, and conducting non-commercial performances.

63 Citizens from Singapore, Japan, Brunei and Mauritius who enter into China to participate in the above commercial or non-commercial activities will require M or F Visa if the duration of their visit exceeds 15 days (or 30 days for those from Mauritius).

64 Processing times usually range from three to five working days following submission of the application to the Chinese Embassy or Consulate nearest the applicants place of residence. The consular officer will decide on the validity, duration of stay, and number of entries, considering the specific circumstances of the applicants.

Short-term assignees

Under the new requirements of the Notice, short-term workers coming to China for 90 days or less for the following reasons should apply for a Z visa: 65
- working with the business partners for technical know-how, research, management and supervisory work;
- conducting training (including coaches and athletes) for sports clubs;
- filming (including advertisements and documentaries);
- performing in fashion shows (including car exhibitions and print ads);
- participating in commercial performances, and;
- other situations as identified by the MHRSS.

If the short-term workers obtaining the Z visa need to stay in China for over 30 days, 66 they would also need to obtain residence permits from the local public security bureaus upon their arrival. Unlike the Z visa for those taking up employment or long-term secondment in China, the **Z visa** for short-term workers is **not renewable upon expiry**.

As the Z visa for short-term workers is not renewable upon expiry, employers 67 and short-term workers should plan and monitor their short-term assignments carefully. If they fail to, they may need to reapply for the Z visa and other permits when the assignment runs over 90 days.

Non-compliance

If foreigners commence work in China without obtaining approval from the relevant 68 authorities, both the individual and the employer may become subject to penalties. In addition, the latest regulations specifically define foreign individual being employed illegally as:
- Working in China without a valid employment permit and residence permit;
- Working outside the location or scope of responsibilities stated in an employment permit;
- Overseas students working outside the scope or timeframe, breaching the administrative regulations by taking part-time jobs while studying in China.

4. Switzerland

What is Switzerland's policy towards corporate immigration?

Switzerland has a dual system for the admission of foreign workers. Gainfully em- 69 ployed nationals from EU and European Free Trade Area (EFTA) states can benefit from the agreement on the free movement of persons. Only a limited number of management level employees, specialists and other qualified employees are admitted into Switzerland from non-EU countries. It is to be noted that only foreigners who actually work and reside on Swiss territory require a work and residence permit. Foreigners who are employed by a Swiss entity, **but who physically work and reside abroad**, do not require a Swiss work and residence permit, even if they are on Swiss payroll and hold a Swiss employment contract.

70 On 9 February 2014, a new constitutional provision was approved by 50.34% of the Swisgs electorate. The provision has the intention of reducing mass immigration into Switzerland and requires that the number of those immigrating into the country be limited . The acceptance of the "mass immigration initiative" by the electorate means that by February 2017 the Swiss Government (so called "Federal Council") implements in a law and in ordinances the new constitutional article 121a and renegotiate/adapt the Agreement on the Free Movement of Persons with the EU.

What is the general process and processing times?

4.1 Non-EU nationals

71 The granting of a work permit for non-EU nationals lies, to a significant extent, in the discretion of the immigration authorities under consideration of the legal framework and the specific circumstances of the application. As a basic principle, only highly skilled and highly qualified employees from non-EU countries may obtain a Swiss work permit and only under the condition that a quota is available. Exception: permits for up to four months or 120 days per year, for which a quota is not necessary.

72 The employing entity is responsible for filing the application with the labor authority responsible for the canton where the foreigner will work. The application has to be approved by the responsible cantonal labor authority, the State Secretariat for Migration and, finally, by the responsible cantonal migration authority. The latter issues the work visa approval, which enables the foreigner to collect the mandatory entry visa at the relevant Swiss representation, proceed with the mandatory post arrival registration and start to work. There are few exceptions where non-EU nationals do not require a work visa in addition to the work authorization (Japan, Singapore, etc.).

73 Non-EU nationals are entitled to start to work only after the post-arrival registration at the relevant commune in Switzerland.

74 The processing time of a non-EU permit application may take around 6 to 8 weeks from the filing date of the application.

75 For 2016, the following work permit quotas are applicable to non-EU nationals:

- short-term L type permits – 4,000;
- long-term B type permits – 2,500.

For 2017, the Federal Council announced on 12 October 2016 that the work permit quotas for Non-EU nationals will be increased as follows: 76
- short-term L type permits – 4,500;
- long-term B type permits – 3,000.

The quotas for Non-EU nationals are allocated annually and are divided in half between the cantons (there is an exact number of quotas for each canton) and the federal government. 77

4.2 EU nationals (with the exception of Croatian nationals)

EU nationals who have signed an employment contract with a Swiss employer may simply register with the commune of residence responsible and start to work right away. 78

In the case of EU nationals **on foreign employment contract** who are **assigned** to Switzerland by their employer as intra-company transferees or as project workers, the application is filed with the labor authority that is responsible for the foreigner's work location in Switzerland. The application has to be pre-approved by the relevant cantonal labor authority prior to the employee being able to start to work. The employee must register with the commune responsible in case of a stay of more than four months or 120 days. 79

The processing time to obtain a work permit for an EU assignee may take around 2 to 3 weeks from the filing date of the application. 80

For 2016, the following work permit quotas apply to EU nationals (with the exception of Croatian nationals) who are assigned to Switzerland as intra-company transferees or project workers by their foreign employer: 81
- short-term L type permits – 2,000;
- long-term B type permits – 250.

These quotas are allocated on a quarterly basis and administered on a federal level. They are not allocated to the cantons like the quotas for non-EU nationals mentioned above. 82

4.3 Croatian nationals

Croatia joined the European Union (EU) on 1 July 2013. Croatia's accession to the EU does not have any immediate bearing on the Agreement on the Free Movement of Persons (AFMP) concluded between Switzerland and the EU. Extension of the AFMP to Croatia was initially negotiated in Protocol III, which provides full free movement of persons for Croatian nationals following a ten-year transition period. The Federal 83

Council signed Protocol III and the corresponding Federal Council Dispatch on 4 March 2016. It now intends to submit Protocol III to the Swiss Parliament for ratification (i.e. legally binding enactment). Until Protocol III comes into effect, Switzerland will continue to apply separate quotas for Croatian nationals; access to the Swiss labor market will remain subject to the provisions of the Foreign Nationals Act. These quotas comprise 50, one-year B permits and 450, short-term L permits.

84 The processing time to obtain a work permit for a Croatian national usually takes around 4 weeks from the filing date of the application.

85 The employing entity submits an application to the cantonal labor authority and, upon receipt of the labor authority's pre-approval; the employee may legally start to working. A post-arrival registration is necessary in case the employee holds a work permit for longer than four months.

What are the most common permit types?

4.4 Online notification ("Meldeverfahren")

86 Online notification enables EU companies to assign employees to Switzerland for a duration of up to 90 days per calendar year without requiring a formal work permit. This on-line notification must usually be completed at least 8 days prior to the assignment start date and is limited to **90 days per assigning entity** (**not per assignee**).

4.5 Short-term residence permit (L permit/Kurzaufenthaltsbewilligung)

87 These are short-term work and residence permits issued for employment or assignment of up to 12 months and extendable for up to 24 months. They are limited by quotas if issued for more than 120 days. After 24 months, L permits can be converted into long-term B type permits. The L permits of Non-EU nationals are "bound" to the sponsoring entity. Also, L permits issued to EU nationals who are not locally hired but on foreign work assignment in Switzerland are bound to a specific position, project and limited by quotas if issued for more than 120 days.

88 Main requirements: employment or assignment contract; in case of Non-EU national or EU assignee, the employee must qualify as a specialist or as management employee; salary and employment conditions must be in line with Swiss requirements.

4.6 Long-term residence permit (B permit or Aufenthaltsbewilligung)

B permits are issued for employment or foreign assignments lasting one year or more. For Non-EU nationals, the permits are issued in general for a duration of one year and it is extendable for two years at the time, subject to each cantonal authority's practice. The B permits of Non-EU nationals are usually "bound" to the sponsoring entity for the first few years, depending on each cantonal authority's practice. For EU nationals on a local Swiss employment contract, the B permit is issued for a duration of five years and guarantees professional and geographical mobility, allowing the holder to get a new job, change the place of work and to become self-employed. 89

Requirements for EU nationals: signature of a Swiss employment contract.

Requirements for Non-EU nationals: employment or assignment contract valid for more than two years; employee must qualify as a specialist or a management or executive employee; the salary and employment conditions must be in line with Swiss requirements; in case of a local hire, the employer must prove that it could not find another suitable candidate on the Swiss and EU labor market. 90

4.7 Settlement permit (C permit/Niederlassungsbewilligung)

This is a long-term settlement permit.

Requirements: The nationals of the following EU countries have a legal entitlement to obtain a C permit after 5 years of continued and uninterrupted residence in Switzerland: 91

- Austria
- Belgium
- Denmark
- France
- Germany
- Greece
- Italy
- Liechtenstein
- Portugal
- Spain
- The Netherlands

Nationals of the following countries may obtain a C permit after 5 years of continued and uninterrupted residence Switzerland, but they do not have a legal entitlement to the C permit: Finland, UK, Ireland, Island, Luxembourg, Monaco, Norway, San Marino, Sweden, The Vatican, as well as by US and Canadian nationals. 92

Nationals of the new EU countries (i.e. Hungary, Poland, Romania etc.) or non-EU nationals may usually obtain a C permit after ten years of Swiss residency and provided they held a B permit for at least the last five years. 93

4.8 Cross border commuter permit (G permit/Grenzgängerbewilligung)

94 G permits are issued to persons working in Switzerland, but who maintain their primary residence in a neighboring country and return home at least once a week.

95 EU/EFTA nationals may live anywhere in the EU/EFTA region and work anywhere in Switzerland provided that they return to their place of residence abroad daily or at least once a week. Non-EU/EFTA nationals must live in the border zone to Switzerland and return home at least once a week.

96 Requirements: Employment contract with a Swiss entity. For Non-EU nationals, employees must have lived in the border zone to Switzerland for at least six months and must qualify as specialists or management employees, with salary and employment conditions in line with Swiss requirements. Further, the employer must prove that it could not find another suitable candidate on the Swiss labor market.

4.9 120-day permit/4-month permit

97 A 120-day or 4-month permit is issued to employees who work in Switzerland for no more than 120 days, spread over a year, or during four consecutive months. Such permits are not restricted by quotas. However, for Non-EU/EFTA nationals, the same requirements apply as for an L or a B permit (qualification as specialist or management employee, salary and working conditions in line with Swiss requirements etc.).

What are the 5–7 typical red flags to watch out for?

98 Only EU nationals locally hired in Switzerland benefit from the Free Movement of Persons (AFMP) concluded between Switzerland and the EU.

99 EU nationals assigned to Switzerland (i.e. **not** working under a Swiss employment contract) require a work permit prior to taking up work in Switzerland. They must qualify as specialists or management employees in order to be eligible for a Swiss work permit. Further restrictions similar to those applicable to Non-EU nationals apply, i.e. pre-check of salary and working conditions, availability of quotas, no legal entitlement, filing of a formal work permit application sponsored by the employing host or home entity.

100 For short-term assignments of EU/EFTA nationals, it is possible to use the online notification instead of obtaining a formal work permit. The use of the online notification is limited to 90 workdays per calendar year and per entity (not per employee).

101 Companies who wish to hire Non-EU nationals must prove that they could not find any employee with a similar profile or professional experience on the Swiss and EU labor market (i.e. **priority of domestic workforce**).

Only management employees, specialists and other qualified employees from Non-EU countries may be admitted into the Swiss labor market. 102

The salary and other terms of employment of non-EU nationals or of EU nationals assigned to Switzerland must be in line with what a Swiss employee in a similar position and with a similar educational and professional background would earn in a similar industry, and in the same particular region of Switzerland the work is to be carried out. 103

Work permits issued to Non-EU/EFTA nationals or to EU/EFTA, assignees for more than 4 months/120 days are subject to **quota restrictions**. 104

5. Singapore

What is Singapore's policy towards corporate immigration?

The city-state of Singapore enjoys one of the world's highest GDP ratios. Throughout 105
the years, the country has adopted an open foreign labor policy to meet the needs of general labor shortage, as well as specific skills shortages. Given Singapore's aspirations to become a major player in the globalized world, the nation's main economic strategy is based on being home to a highly skilled workforce. In the recent years, changes have been observed as the government has attempted to cap foreign workers at one-third of the labor force.

Corporate immigration generally involves inflows of skilled work permit, re- 106
ferred to as "foreign talent" in both government and public discourse. According to the statistics released by the National Population and Talent Division in its annual Population Brief Report for 2015, skilled workers and professionals account for about 22% of Singapore's total non-resident workforce of 1.63 million workers.

What is the general process and processing times?

An EP application must be submitted within three (3) months from the closing date 107
of the job advertisement on the WDA jobs bank. The same is not required for S Pass application. EP and S Pass applications are submitted to the Ministry of Manpower ("MOM") either online or manually. The most common method is via online submission through a portal called the EP Online ("EPOL"), which allows employers and third party service providers to perform pass application submission, issuance and cancellation. When the EPOL account is set-up, the pass application can then be submitted to the MOM for consideration.

Once approved, the successful applicant must be in Singapore at the time the 108
pass is issued. Thereafter, to obtain the biometric pass card, applicant is required to appear in person at the Employment Pass Services Centre at a pre-arranged appointment time to complete necessary photo-imaging and fingerprinting formalities.

109 The processing time for pass applications submitted via the EPOL is generally 1 to 2 weeks, as compared to approximately 5 weeks if submitted manually. The processing time for some work pass applications may be longer if the foreign employee had previously held Singapore Permanent Residence ("PR") or Singapore Citizenship (e.g. may require a longer processing time of 1 to 2 months or more). It is also important to note that supporting documents in foreign language requires English translation and some documents may require verification by external agencies (e.g. some may take approximately 30 working days for verification to be obtained). As such, longer time may be required to obtain the relevant supporting documents prior to the submission of EP application.

What are the most common permit types?

110 The most common work passes that allow foreign nationals to live and work in Singapore include the Employment Pass (EP) and S Pass.

111 The EP category is designed for foreign professionals, managers and executives with a job offer in Singapore that earns them a fixed monthly salary of at least SGD 3,300. From 1 January 2017, new EP applicants will require an offer with a fixed monthly salary of at least SGD 3,600, depending on their qualifications and experience. More experienced applicants are expected to have higher salaries to qualify for an EP.

112 As part of the EP application procedure, the company may be required to advertise the job opening on the Jobs Bank, an online job portal administered by the Workforce Development Agency ("WDA"). The advertisement must be open to Singaporeans and run for at least fourteen (14) days. The EP is issued up to two (2) years for first time candidates and renewals are issued up to three (3) years. No foreign worker levy or quota is required for the employer.

113 The S Pass is a type of work pass designed for mid-level skilled workers (e.g. technicians) who earn a fixed monthly salary of at least SGD 2,200 with acceptable qualifications/certificates and work experience. Employers of S Pass holders will need to pay a foreign levy. The levy rates vary for each industry sector; there are currently five sectors, namely: construction, process, marine, manufacturing and service. The rates are tiered so that those who hire close to the maximum quota will pay a higher levy. The levy liability starts from the day the S Pass is issued and ends when the pass is cancelled or expires. The number of S Pass employees that a company can hire is also limited by quota, or Dependency Ratio Ceiling. Employers are also required to provide and maintain medical insurance for the S pass holders for the duration of their employment in Singapore with the given employer. The insurance coverage must be at least SGD 15,000 per year and cover inpatient care and outpatient surgery.

114 Additionally, EP and S Pass holders who have a fixed monthly salary of at least SGD 5,000 are eligible for a Dependent's Pass for their spouse and children.

What are the 5–7 typical red flags to watch out for?

The Fair Consideration Framework ("FCF") is part of the Government's overall effort to strengthen the Singaporean core in the workforce. The FCF applies to all companies in Singapore. FCF requires all companies to have mandatory posting of job advertisements in the WDA's portal prior to submission of an EP application. Employers are still expected to consider Singaporeans fairly for jobs even if an exemption to the advertising requirement is applicable. Companies must comply with various regulations stipulated by the Tripartite Alliance for Fair and Progressive Employment Practices ("TAFEP"), such as not stating a nationality, age, race, religion, language, gender, marital status or family responsibility preference. 115

In April 2016, the MOM further refined the EP processing criteria. Apart from assessing the individual-related criteria, the MOM will now also look into three additional factors that are company-related. These factors include: 116

1. The company's proportion of Singaporeans compared to industry average.
2. The company's commitment to hire and develop Singaporeans.
3. The company's importance to Singapore's economy and society

The assessment will be carried out by the TAFEP. Those companies found to be weak in all three criteria are placed under the "Watch List". Subsequently, if they do not pass the review held six months later, their work pass privileges might be curtailed. 117

Other typical red flags relating to potential longer processing time – or even unsuccessful work pass application outcome – could include applicants having criminal record; refused entry or deporting from any country; academic qualifications obtained from certain countries (e.g. India and People's Republic of China) subject to additional verification (e.g. submission of full transcripts and mark sheets (transcripts) or verification proof of academic qualification certificates). 118

Same sex spouses and partners are not recognized in Singapore. They have to obtain an appropriate pass on their own merits to stay in Singapore (e.g. EP if they are working in Singapore). 119

6. Russia

What is Russia's policy towards corporate immigration?

The immigration policy of the Russian government aims to protect local employees and maintaining the workforce balance within the country. There are no restrictions on how many foreign employees can work in a given Russian company or how long they can be employed in Russia. However, restrictions are in place regarding the types of activities in which foreign employees can be engaged. For instance, foreign 120 nationals may not work in public service. Also, the Russian Government is entitled to establish statutory thresholds for the share of foreign employees in the entities engaged in certain spheres for each calendar year (such thresholds may be established for particular regions of Russia).

121 The procedure for obtaining work authorization documents for immigrants coming from both visa and non-visa countries is not simple and in practice takes at least 3.5 months for those coming to Russia from visa countries and at least a month from non-visa country. However, recent trends in Russian migration and employment legislation show that the Russian government intends to promote further a more effective and flexible policy for the category of foreign employees who are considered highly qualified specialists ("**HQS**").

What is the general process and processing times?

122 The general process would first depend on the citizenship of the foreign national in question. Thus, the procedure of formalizing work authorization documents for expatriates entering Russia on a visa basis (e.g., citizens of the United Kingdom, the United States and most European countries) and those for expatriates entering Russia on a non-visa basis (e.g. citizens of Tajikistan, Ukraine, Uzbekistan and some other former Soviet republics of the Union) are different. There are also special preferences for the citizens of the countries that are members of the Eurasian Economic Union. Please find more details in this regard below.

(a) Foreign nationals entering Russia on visa basis

123 The general process of formalizing work authorization documents for foreign nationals entering Russia on visa basis (e.g. citizens of the United Kingdom, the United States and most European countries) includes the following stages:

1. The prospective employer of a foreign national applies for a quota (i.e. reserves the right to employ foreign nationals with the particular citizenship at particular positions). The quota application shall be filed in the year *preceding* the year in which foreign nationals are going to be employed. This stage may be omitted, provided that the respective foreign nationals are employed in quota-exempt positions. NOTE: the statutory list of such positions is updated on an annual basis;
2. the employer informs the local employment state agency of its vacant positions and then looks for suitable local candidates during the subsequent one-month period. Only if no suitable local candidates have been found may the employer initiate the application process for employment permit;
3. the employer obtains the employment permit. The employment permit will authorize the employer to employ foreign nationals with the particular citizenship at the particular positions;

4. the employer applies for a single-entry work visa invitation for the foreign national and a work permit in the latter's name;
5. the employer collects the single-entry work visa invitation from the immigration authorities and sends it to the foreign national via courier mail;
6. the foreign national applies with Russian consular authorities outside Russia for a single-entry work visa. Upon obtainment of such visa the foreign national enters Russia and passes:
   - applicable medical tests
   - exam on the command of the Russian language and on knowledge of the basics of Russian legislation and history;
7. the employer collects the individual work permit in the foreign national's name from the immigration authorities (regular work permit), the employer and the foreign national execute the relevant employment contract;
8. the expatriate employee (the foreign national) commences his or her employment with the employer;
9. the single-entry work visa of the expatriate employee is converted into a multiple-entry work visa.

In practice, the time frame for undergoing the steps above (from informing the employment authorities on the available vacant positions until obtainment of the multiple entry work visa for the expatriate employee) may take up to 6 months. 124

(b) Foreign nationals entering Russia on a non-visa basis

The general process of formalizing work authorization documents for foreign nationals entering Russia on a non-visa basis includes the following stages. 125

1. the prospective expatriate employee enters Russia and passes:
   - applicable medical tests;
   - exam on the command of the Russian language and on knowledge of the basics of Russian legislation and history;
2. the prospective expatriate employee applies for a work patent[24] and makes an advance payment to the state budget of the respective region of employment in the consideration of his or her personal income tax to be accrued in the future. The amount of the advanced payment depends on the fixed monthly rate established by the respective Russian region and the planned duration of the employment;
3. the prospective expatriate employee collects his or her work patent, enters into an employment agreement with the employer and commences his or her em-

24 In Russia a work patent issued to non-visa expatriate employees is an equivalent of the work permit issued to visa expatriate employees.

ployment. NOTE: immigration authorities shall be provided a copy of the employment agreement.

In practice, the steps above may take up to 1.5 months.

(c) Citizens of the countries that are members of the Eurasian Economic Union

126 As for the citizens of the countries that are members of the Eurasian Economic Union (Armenia, Belarus, Kazakhstan and Kyrgystan), employing such citizens does not require formalizing employment permits, work permits and patents, so no processing time applies for these foreign nationals.

(d) Highly qualified specialist (HQS)

127 Both visa and non-visa expatriate employees are eligible for simplified procedure of formalizing the migration permissive documents. This procedure includes the following stages:

- the prospective employer and the foreign national sign the employment contract;
- the employer applies for a multiple-entry work visa invitation for the prospective expatriate employee and that employee's highly qualified specialist (HQS) work permit. That type of permit is issued in the name of that foreign national;
- the employer collects the mentioned visa invitation and sends it to the foreign national by courier mail;
- the foreign national applies to the Russian consular authorities outside Russia for a multiple entry work visa. Upon obtainment of such visa the foreign national enters Russia and collects his or her work permit in person;
- the expatriate employee commences his or her employment with the employer.

128 For non-visa expatriates, the procedure is even simpler, as no work visa invitations and visas shall be formalized for such expatriates – only obtainment of the HQS work permit is required.

129 In practice, the time frame for formalizing the work permit and the invitation for a multiple entry work visa for a highly qualified specialist is approximately one month. The statutory time frame for processing the work permit of a highly qualified specialist by the authorities is 14 working days.

What are the most common permit types?

130 **Regular work permit:**

- there is a quota for issuance such work permits;
- employer has to obtain the company's employment permit;

- the permit is issued for the maximum term of one year;
- the work permit may be valid in one Russian region only;
- foreign national has to pass exams on command of Russian and knowledge of basics of Russian history and politics;
- foreign national has to pass medical tests in Russia.

Work patent: 131
- there is no quota for issuance of work patent;
- employer does not have to obtain the company's employment permit;
- the term of patent is one year (this term is subject to extension for one additional year);
- the work patent is valid in one Russian region only;
- foreign national has to pass exams on command of Russian and knowledge of basics of Russian history and politics;
- foreign national has to pass medical tests in Russia.

HQS: 132
- HQS work permit may be issued to a foreign national whom an employer in Russia is willing to put on a Russian company payroll, with the monthly salary of no less than RUB 167,000 (gross);
- there is no quota for issuance of HQS work permits;
- employer does not have to obtain the company's employment permit;
- the term of the HQS work permit may be up to three years;
- the HQS work permit may be valid in more than one Russian region;
- foreign national does not have to pass exams on command of Russian and knowledge of basics of Russian history and politics;
- foreign national does not have to pass medical tests in Russia.

What are the 5–7 typical red flags to watch out for?

- notification of the immigration authorities on employment contract conclusion – 3 working days;[25] 133
- the purpose of the visit of the foreign national should correspond to the scope of activities that he or she actually performs in Russia;[26]
- as a general rule each foreign national should be registered at the address of his place of stay (work) within seven working days from the date of his or her arri-

25 This requirement is applicable for ALL foreign employees, including those who can work in Russia without work permits.

26 E.g., a foreign national staying in Russian under business visa may not work in Russia in most cases.

val into Russia (HQS are exempted from this requirement during the first 90 days of their stay in Russia);

- in case of change of the passport details the foreign employee should apply for the correction of the work permit within seven working days from the date of obtainment of the new passport, or the date of arrival to Russia if the passport was obtained outside Russia;
- in case a foreign national committed two or more administrative violations, he or she may be denied entry into Russia during the term of three years;
- the employer should generally arrange for medical insurance (including medical and emergency care) for the entire period of foreign employee's employment and specify the details of the insurance policy in the employment contract.

7. Brazil

What is Brazil's policy towards corporate immigration?

134 The number of foreign citizens willing to come to Brazil in order to study or work is steadily increasing. Because of this, the Brazilian Ministry of Labor and Employment granted nearly 7,400 work authorizations to foreigners from all over the world in the first quarter of 2016, the majority being Europeans, Asians and North Americans.

135 Nonetheless, the granting of Brazilian working visas is on condition of the fulfilment of several requirements established by Brazilian immigration law, and the visa application process is only approved after careful analysis of the relevant documentation by the Ministry of Labor and Employment. The current process notwithstanding, the federal government is working on softening the rules, as indicated by *Decree no. 8757*, published in the *Official Gazette* on May 11, 2016, which alters several procedures of the *Decree no. 86715, 1981,* related to the legal status of foreigners in Brazil.

What is the general process and processing time?

136 After gathering all necessary documents to apply for the most suitable working visa, the corresponding visa application is submitted to the Immigration Department of the Brazilian Ministry of Labor and Employment. Under the sole discretion of the Immigration Department, typically takes 30 to 45 days to grant or deny the request, or require additional information or documentation. It is essential to know that this process is mandatory for all wishing to work in Brazil. Indeed, foreign applicants are only allowed to start working after entering Brazil with the corresponding working visa, which he or she may is collect at a chosen Brazilian Consulate or Embassy abroad.

What are the most common permit types?

The main immigration permission categories applied in Brazil are: 137

Temporary working visa under a local Labor relationship:

The Temporary Working visa based on a local employment relationship entitles the 138
foreigner to work in Brazil under an employment relationship with a Brazilian company for a period of two years. After the end of this term, a transformation of such visa into a Permanent Working visa may be required.

Beyond needing to conclude an employment agreement, for the application for 139
a Temporary Working Visa based on an employment relationship, it will be also necessary to present to the Brazilian Immigration authorities a set of documents from the foreigner. This primarily includes providing evidence of meeting a minimum professional experience and educational level in the same area of the assignments that he or she will perform in Brazil. Companies operating in Brazil will need to demonstrate its lawful incorporation and validity, as well as the powers of its legal representative who has executed the employment agreement, among others.

01-year Temporary Technical Visa:

This type of visa is appropriate for foreigner workers who come to Brazil to render 140
technical services, transfer technology or render technical assistance. Such foreign workers retain their bond with their foreign employer and are not allowed to receive any remuneration in Brazil. This type of visa is valid for one year, and is extendable for an additional year.

Among other requirements, the application for the one-year Temporary Techni- 141
cal Visa requires that a technical agreement or convention entered into by and between the foreign employer of the employee and the Brazilian company in which he/she will render his/her services be presented to Brazilian immigration authorities of a.

Please note that the purpose for this type of visa is the sharing of technical 142
knowledge with Brazilian employees. Therefore, another mandatory document of the process is a training program explaining, in detail, the scope, methodology and expected outcomes from the training to be provided in Brazil.

Permanent working visa for individual foreign investors:

This visa is applicable for foreign nationals who wish to furnish their own funds for 143
investment activity in Brazil. For the application of this type of permanent working visa, the foreign national directly invests a minimum amount of BRL (Brazilian Real) 500,000 into a Brazilian company, or the equivalent in any foreign currency.

In exceptional cases, the National Immigration Council, under certain specific 144
and discretionary conditions, may grant a permanent working visa for a foreign national whose amount of investment is between BRL 150,000 and 500,000, or the equivalent in any foreign currency. According to Brazilian immigration law, "the

investment must result in an increase in the employment and income in Brazil, as well as in the productivity, through the assimilation of technology and fundraising for specific sectors." For this purpose, another mandatory document for the visa application is an investment plan.

Permanent working visa for executive officers or directors:

145 The Permanent Working Visa is applicable to foreign candidates who will:
- assume the position of manager, administrator or corporate officer of a Brazilian company;
- be responsible for the performance of company managerial activities;
- hold legal representation and signatory powers for the company.

146 For the application of this type of visa, the foreigner will have to have been previously appointed as a statutory officer in the company's by-Laws or other related corporate document, duly registered at the Registry of Commerce, subjecting his or her authority to the obtaining the corresponding Permanent Working Visa.

147 Moreover, one of the mandatory requirements for the application of such type of visa includes providing evidence to Brazilian immigration authorities of a direct investment into the Brazilian company for which the foreign national will perform the managerial activities. The payment of at least BRL 600,000.00 has to have been made by one of the company's foreign shareholders or the equivalent amount in other currency **per visa application**, which is duly registered at the Brazilian Central Bank Information System ("SISBACEN").

Professional Exchange Visa:

148 Under the aforementioned type of visa, undergraduate or recently graduate foreign students are allowed to work in Brazil in a short-term basis, in order to improve their educational background and obtain professional and cultural experience, for a maximum period of 01 (one) year, not extendable.

Professional Training Visa:

149 This visa is suitable to foreigners, with labor bound with the foreign company, who wish to have professional training in the company's Brazilian subsidiary or head office, both of them necessarily part of the same economic group. It is only valid for 01 year, not extendable.

What are the 5–7 typical red flags to watch out for?

150
- Foreign holders of technical working visas are not able to render services to any company other than the one that sponsored the visa.
- The business visa is suitable only for foreigners who wish to come to Brazil in order to take part in workshops, meet clients and other non-productive activi-

ties. The holder of a business visa is not allowed to have a working routine in Brazil, such as for example, have time to arrive at the company in the morning and leave in the afternoon, have a personal desk, computer, phone line, perform managerial tasks, give or receive training, provide technical assistance or perform any other work-related activities, under the risk of been deported. In addition, the holder of a business visa is not allowed to receive any kind of remuneration in Brazil.

- The Brazilian immigration authorities follow objective criteria established by the Brazilian Immigration Law. Nevertheless, such authorities are allowed a certain degree of discretion in concrete cases.
- With regard to complicated cases, it is possible to submit, along with the officially required documents, other documents or a petition explaining any exceptional situation to the Brazilian immigration authorities.
- There is a minimum salary requirement for some specific categories. As per Brazilian immigration laws, foreign nationals who hold a temporary or permanent working visa and take part of an intra-company transfer must receive in Brazil an equal or higher remuneration than they received abroad. On the other hand, if the foreign national is hired from the market (not an infra-company transfer), his or her salary must be equal to or higher than the salary paid to a Brazilian employee holding the same position in the Brazilian company.
- If a Brazilian company wishes to apply for a Brazilian working visa for a certain foreign national, it must justify the hiring of such foreign national by proving that the individual possesses certain skills and knowledge that could not be found in any other potential Brazilian candidate.
- Nevertheless, for the purpose of applying for the temporary working visa for a foreign national before the Brazilian immigration authorities, the Brazilian company must provide evidence that at least two-thirds of its work force is composed by Brazilian employees and that the same proportion is observed in terms of payroll for Brazilian employees.
- Brazilian consulates require the presentation of certificates of criminal records in order to issue visas that were approved by the Brazilian Ministry of Labor and Employment. In this sense, criminal convictions may jeopardize the obtainment of immigration permissions, depending on the evaluation of the consulate.

Part 2
Employment Law

I. Introduction to German employment law

1. German employment by numbers

In May 2016, approximately 43.5[27] million people with residence in Germany were employed, making Germany the EU country with the second highest employment rate. The majority of the regular employees – those subject to compulsory social insurance contributions – are employed in fulltime, approximately 23 million people.[28] 1

In 2014, 4.62 million people were employed with fixed-term and 30.85 million with a permanent contracts.[29] 2

The average gross remuneration of a full-time employee was 3,612 EUR per month in 2015. In the eastern part of Germany, however, employees receive a lower average monthly remuneration than in the western part of the country, averaging, 2,886 EUR gross monthly in the 2015.[30] 3

In April 2015, about 1.9 million jobs earned the German minimum wage.

2. Social security system and 50/50 split

There are five key elements to the German social security system: 4

- Unemployment insurance
- Pension insurance
- Health insurance
- Accident insurance and
- Nursing insurance

Based on gross salary, monthly premiums range from 3% for unemployment insurance to 18.7% pension insurance (status January 2016). 5

The cost is principally divided in half, with the employer paying the one half and the employee the other, a 50/50 split. A few exceptions do exist, however. German regulations mandate what at least superficially appears at to be a rather sensi- 6

27 https://www.destatis.de/DE/PresseService/Presse/Pressemitteilungen/2016/01/PD16_025_122.html.

28 https://www.destatis.de/DE/ZahlenFakten/GesamtwirtschaftUmwelt/Arbeitsmarkt/Erwerbstaetigkeit/TabellenBeschaeftigungsstatistik/Strukturdaten.html.

29 http://de.statista.com/statistik/daten/studie/152407/umfrage/befristet-und-unbefristet-erwerbstaetige-in-deutschland/.

30 https://www.destatis.de/DE/ZahlenFakten/GesamtwirtschaftUmwelt/VerdiensteArbeitskosten/VerdiensteVerdienstunterschiede/Tabellen/Bruttomonatsverdienste.html.

ble exception for employees without children. Those workers are required to pay an extra 25% for their nursing care insurance premium, one of the reasons being to financially relieve the state of being responsible for childless people who require nursing assistance later in life. Also, for the health insurance, beyond the 50/50 split, there may be an additional contribution, averaging 1.1%, subject to decision of the health insurance provider.

3. Annual paid leave

7 Weekly working hours vary by industry sector and by location, but mostly range between 37 to 40 hours weekly. The legal minimum paid holiday entitlement is 20 work days per annum for employees working in a five-day week. Collective bargaining, trade union and other employment agreements often increase this, with most entitlements to vacation ranging between 25 and 30 days per annum. Management and older employees are often entitled to as many as 32 days of vacation time per annum.

8 Public holidays vary from 10 to 13 days annually depending on in which of the 16 federal states (Bundesländer) in which the employee is employed.[31]

4. Specifics of German Employment Law

Basic principles of employment German employment law

9 German law does not codify law in a singular "Employment Act". Instead, one finds employment matters addressed in several different acts. Additionally and for many familiar with Roman law traditions, surprisingly, case law has a tremendous impact on German employment law. Decisions handed down by German labor courts – especially those from the German Federal Labor Court– play a major role in patching the holes found in employment-related statutes. In 2014 alone, 502,272[32] cases were pending before local labor law courts, 24,895[33] in front of the state courts of appeal and 2,313[34] in front of the Federal Labor Law Court.[35]

31 For detail on this topic in English, see: http://www.timeanddate.com/holidays/germany/.

32 http://www.bmas.de/SharedDocs/Downloads/DE/PDF-Statistiken/Ergebnisse-Statistik--Arbeitsgerichtsbarkeit-2014.pdf?__blob=publicationFile&v=2.

33 http://www.bmas.de/SharedDocs/Downloads/DE/PDF-Statistiken/Ergebnisse-Statistik--Arbeitsgerichtsbarkeit-2014.pdf?__blob=publicationFile&v=2.

34 http://www.bundesarbeitsgericht.de/download/jahresbericht_2015.pdf.

35 http://www.bundesarbeitsgericht.de/download/jahresbericht_2015.pdf.

As one looks at German employment law regulations, one thing becomes obvious: its principle objective is the protection of employees working within the country's borders. The schematic for breaking down how these protections work is best explained as a hierarchical pyramid: 10

As one might imagine, if the issue is located on the top of the hierarchical pyramid, its jurisprudential significance is correspondingly higher with respect to German employment laws. As with most things in law, there are exceptions, and the so-called German favorability principle **(Günstigkeitsprinzip)**, the practice of deviating from a given collective bargaining agreement for the employee's benefit is one. This principle is simpler than it may sound to non-Germans: the provision which is more beneficial to the employee remains in force, regardless of the level in the hierarchy, as long as the given provision is valid law. Such deviations from statutory regulations, work agreements or collective bargain agreements that favor employee interests are nearly always permissible. 11

Despite such favorability of the employee, employers, of course, still enjoy flexibility with respect to certain elements of the employment relationship. For example, employers retain the comprehensive right to direct employees regarding working times, location and the work to be performed. The only viable exceptions are those regarding issues that are regulated by a given employment agreement, works council agreement or the collective bargaining agreement. 12

For those unfamiliar with a works council, it is worth noting briefly here what they are. A works council is a body elected by all employees at the company. They have co-determination rights, the right to have input on hiring, firing and other 13 workplace-related matters. A works council, it should be noted, is not a trade union, as a works council is internal and the trade union external to the company. Indeed, a trade union operating in Germany, as in many other places in world, may represent more than one company. That is one of the reasons the works council is so vital in the eyes of German employment law: it places above all the interest of the workers at the site or company they are elected to represent and in certain circumstances may not be concerned with what is transpiring in a particular union. That said, both unions and work councils do work together on many issues.

Individual Employment Agreements and Collective Bargaining Agreements

14 Individual employment agreements between employers and employees represent the main legal source regarding employment relationships. It is customary for all employees at all levels to have a signed contract in Germany. In this respect, most employers use a standard employment contract for all of their employees in order to make their HR process more manageable. These documents are generally governed by the German Act Governing Standard Business Conditions (Gesetz zur Regelung des Rechts der Allgemeinen Geschäftsbedingungen – AGB-Gesetz).

15 A works agreement (**Betriebsvereinbarung**), on the other hand, represents an agreement between employers and the given works council. They regulate work conditions where no collective bargaining agreement (**Tarifvertrag**) exists, or may act as an additional level of protection of workers. Works agreements directly influence employment relationships, since they have an immediate and binding effect on individual employment relationships as statutory law would. Thus, employers do not have to seek negotiations with individual employees. For example, if the given company wants to initiate reduced working hours, it can conclude a works agreement with the works council that affects all the employment relationships for employees that fall within the works agreement's scope.

16 As for the **collective bargaining agreement**, an employers' association or an individual employer negotiates and concludes a contract with a trade union. These types of agreements regulate a sizeable number of crucial working condition matters, such as weekly working hours, annual leave and notice periods. German law neither requires employers to sign collective bargaining agreements nor join employer associations nor make use of those agreements. However, collective labor agreements that are generally binding set general standards for application to all employment contracts within the scope of such an agreement.

II. Definitions

To correctly determine the consequences of international postings of employees from an employment law perspective, understanding the different types of postings of employees is of great importance. 1

1. Business Trip

There is no standard legal definition for the term business trip (*Dienstreise/Geschäftsreise*). The German Federal Labor Court defines a business trip to be a trip to a place outside of the regular work site where official business is to be carried out. This definition requires that the employee performs a work-related task at the other place. With a business trip, one refers to a stay of no more than three months, be it domestic or abroad. Note: business trips have no effect on an employment contract. 2

Business trips are in the framework of the employer's instruction right (*Direktionsrecht*) if covered by the job description or any other contractual regulations. 3

2. Assignment

There is no legal definition of an assignment. 4

An assignment of an employee can be for a long term, which is usually between one and five years or for a short term, which is usually between three and twelve months. A posting of employees is based on the employee's existing employment contract, and the employee is to be working for the German employer abroad or one of its foreign subsidiaries due to a special contractual agreement based on instruction the employer has given the employee.

An assignment agreement is the legal basis for temporarily assigning (posting) an employee to work abroad. There are different contract models that should be determined by the particular situation and depend on the length and type of the employment abroad. In other words, the choice of a suitable contract is contingent on the length of stay, the work to be carried out as well as the position and situation in which the posting of the employee takes place. 5

3. Project Work

Project work is a kind of short term assignment and usually performed by employees who need to work at a client's site for a period of one month to a longer period. In cases of project work it is always important to comply with all immigration require- 6 ments and to avoid any risk of the project work being considered as illegal personnel lending.

4. Split Employment

7 In case an employee would work at several entities in different countries at the same time, it is recommended to agree on a split employment contract. With each entity, an employment contract needs to be concluded, i.e. the employee has two or more part-time employment contracts which need to correlate with each other with regard to among others, the amount of annual leave, salary, taxes and social security. Furthermore, in these cases, it is extremely important to keep an eye on the correct management regarding a potential risk to create a permanent establishment.

III. Applicable Law for international assignments to Germany

As soon as an employee/assignee is working in a different country than his home country, i.e. Germany, he or she gets in contact with the foreign jurisdiction as well. 1

At a first glance, it does not seem clear which jurisdiction would be applicable to the respective employment situation. Since each jurisdiction has different issues to consider, problems can arise regarding the applicability. 2

In order to have clarity regarding the applicable legal provisions, the conflict-of-law rules apply. 3

For all contracts which were concluded after Dec 17, 2009, the so-called Rome-I regulation applies (Regulation (EC) No 593/2008 – the law applicable on contractual obligations). For contracts concluded before this date, the provisions of Art. 27 et seq. of the EGBGB (Introductory Law to the Civil Code) apply. 4

In the following, we will provide a short overview on the applicable law according to the Rome I-regulation. 5

1. Choice of law

Art. 8 Sec. 1 Rome I-regulation in connection with Art. 3 Rome I Regulation states that in general, the parties can agree on the applicable law autonomously. The (explicit) choice can be made either for the complete contract or for parts of the contract. An implied choice of law is also conceivable, e.g. by referring to a collective bargaining agreement or to specific legal provisions or company agreements. 6

In any case, the general possibility of choosing the applicable law is subject to restrictions. 7

Art. 8 Sec. 1 Sentence 2 of the Rome I Regulation states that the employee shall not be deprived of certain mandatory employee rights which would have been applicable had no choice of law been made. Furthermore, it is required that this (applicable) legal system would have been more advantageous. 8

Mandatory provisions according to German employment law are: 9

- Dismissal protection
- Working time
- Minimum holiday entitlement
- Control of terms and conditions
- Post-contractual restraint
- Principle of equality/prohibition of discrimination
- Continued remuneration in case of illness
- Fixed-term contracts
- Occupational safety

2. No choice of law

10 In case no choice of law has been made, the employment/assignment is either subject to the national law of the country, where the employee regularly conducts his work even if he is assigned temporarily to a different country **or** where the employing entity has its establishment in case the employee does not usually works in the same country. An exception applies if all the circumstances of the case imply a deeper connection to a (third) country.

3. Overriding mandatory rules

11 Even if a foreign law is applicable in accordance with the aforementioned, there are certain provisions of German law which are still applicable due to Art. 9 Rome I-Regulation, such as dismissal protection of disabled and pregnant employees, occupational safety, paid annual leave, principle of equality or employee leasing. On the other hand, rules on general dismissal protection, transfer of enterprise provisions (Sec. 613a Civil Code) and generally applicable collective bargaining agreements are no overriding mandatory rules.

4. Nachweisgesetz (German Act on notification of conditions governing an employment relationship)

12 The German Act on notification of conditions governing an employment relationship mainly stipulates that the following conditions need to be fixed in writing (electronical form is not sufficient) in case the employee is to be posted abroad longer than one month:
- duration of the posting/assignment;
- currency of the remuneration which will be paid;
- additional remuneration and benefits paid;
- conditions regarding to the return of the employee.

5. Arbeitnehmerentsendegesetz (German Employee Posting Act)

13 The German Employee Posting Act has mandatory application between an employer with headquarters abroad and his/her employee within the scope of a collective bargaining agreement. One requirement is that the business or business unit is operating in the spirit of the framework of the collective bargaining agreement for the given industry. The domestic employer has to allow at least for the working conditions applicable to and afforded under the collective bargaining agreement in the

given industry. The German Employee Posting Act further offers a legal framework for setting the minimum wage in a collective bargaining agreement for a given sector binding, regardless of whether the employer is headquartered domestically or abroad.

The German Employee Posting Act only applies to certain industries which are construction, commercial cleaning, letter delivery and laundry and security services, specialized mine work, waste management and educational and training services. 14

6. German minimum wage

Since January 1, 2015, Germany has a minimum wage according to the German Minimum Wage Act. In 2015 the general minimum wage started at 8,50€ per hour and this was increased to 8,84€, effective as of January 1st 2017. Besides this provision, there are different minimum wages in certain industries. During the transition period until the end of 2017, the minimum wage in certain industries can be below the statutory requirement. After the transition period, other minimum wage provisions from e.g. collective bargaining agreements may only be applied if the wage is higher than the statutory minimum wage. 15

The minimum wage is mostly not of importance in cases of international assignments. In order to obtain the relevant work and residence permit, it is required to prove that the salary is comparable to those of equivalent (German) employees and this mostly is much higher than the minimum wage (i.e. for highly qualified employees who apply for a Blue Card-EU: 49,600 EUR gross annually). 16

IV. Contractual Set-Up

1 For both inbound and outbound assignments, practice has shown that two different ways for the contractual set-up of an assignment are being used by international companies:

- The employee remains an employee of the foreign (home) company and next to his foreign employment contract the individual receives a secondment agreement. This agreement regulates the terms and conditions for the time of the assignment to Germany but the employee is still an employee of the foreign company.

OR

- The employment contract in the home country is dormant for the time of the assignment and the employee receives a fixed term local contract with the host company.

2 A legally compliant contractual set-up is always required since the instruction right of the employer does not suffice to assign an employee to another country by way of a unilateral declaration. There might be exceptions if the original home country employment contract provides for a possibility of an international assignment of the employee or if the assignment shall be of a very short term (in this case it would be covered by the German right to instruct its employees).

1. Active home country employment contract

3 The first option is to keep the home country contract active and agree on an additional agreement regarding the assignment. In this case, the home country employment contract remains unchanged while the terms and conditions for the duration of the assignment are being determined in an assignment (secondment) agreement. This can be regarded as a modification of the existing home country employment contract.

4 In this case, the assignee needs to remain integrated into the organization of the home country and follow instructions from the home country employer for the whole period of assignment.

5 Usually, there is no contract with the host company. There should be confirmation as to whether this set-up is compliant from an immigration perspective since some countries require a local employment contract for the issuance of a visa/work permit.

2. Dormant home country employment contract

The second option is a two-contract-model: the home country employment contract will be made dormant for a fixed-term (the duration of the assignment) and a local employment contract with fixed term will be concluded with the host company as employer in the host country. Such a contract is subject to the laws of the host country. 6

The employee will be embedded into the organization of the host company and will receive his/her work instructions solely from the host country employer. As a result, the employee might have – among others- a new superior, a different remuneration system and depending on the host country – a lower or higher holiday entitlement. 7

3. Other contractual set-ups

Beside the common contractual set-ups, an assignment can also be subject to other combined contractual set-ups. 8

For instance, the home country contract can be still active or only partially dormant, or an "assignment agreement" will only be concluded with the home company while there is no contract with the host company. 9

An employee can also be partly assigned. It is important that in these cases the provisions of the different contracts need to correspond to each other. Furthermore, in case of termination of the employment, it is important to have an overview over all existing employment relationships. In case of doubt, each employment relationship needs to be terminated separately. 10

In case the employee shall work in two countries for two employers (usually group companies) at the same time, it is recommendable to agree on a split employment contract. This kind of contract can be legally set up by either two part time contracts or as a partial assignment. Usually, there will be two separate employment agreements, each of these as a part-time employment contract. It is important that both contracts are harmonized with each other, especially with respect to the amount of annual leave, public holidays and regarding social security and tax. Having too many part-time employment relationships at the same time should be avoided. 11

V. Personnel Leasing

1 When looking at sending employees to Germany, or when sending employees from Germany to a foreign country, the question of personnel leasing – particularly the illegal leasing of personnel – becomes very relevant. Generally speaking, every international placement of personnel would be considered personnel leasing at least under German regulations. It all comes down to one employer in the home country 'leasing' personnel to another employer in the host country. In the following we will explain personnel leasing according to German regulations and when it is applicable to international assignments. Please keep in mind that German regulations mainly apply when sending personnel to Germany but should also be looked at when sending German employees to other countries.

1. Definition: explanation of personnel leasing

2 The leasing of personnel finds its legal basis in the German Temporary Employment Act (*Arbeitnehmerüberlassungsgesetz – AÜG*). According to the provisions of this act, the leasing of employees occurs if the employer (lender) allocates an employee to a third party (borrower) on the basis of an employee leasing agreement. With this arrangement, the lent employee remains in an employment relationship with the lender during the time that he/she is completely integrated into the borrower's organization, in order to work for the promotion of the company in accordance with the ideas and aims of the borrower and its employees. During the lending out period, the leased out employee is subject to the borrower's right to instruct his/her employees (*Weisungsrecht*).

2. Applicability to international assignments

3 In case the work assignment takes place between affiliated companies, it is irrelevant whether the employee is leased or borrowed from the dependent company. For this kind of "personnel lease", no permission of the labor authority is required. The commercial leasing can only be temporary. A key point is whether the employee should return to his original company or if she or he leaves the company for good. In case of an assignment between affiliated companies, the exemption from the obligation to have permission granted only applies if the employee has not been employed for the sole purpose of being immediately posted to another (group) company.

4 An employee is required to work abroad for a third party at the request of the employer if the conditions of commercial leasing exist. In addition, the German employer has to conclude a service or work contract with the third party that comports with German norms.

In case of outbound employees, the foreign regulations regarding employee leasing – if existing at all – need to be taken into consideration. 5

3. Outlook – upcoming changes

The German government has decided on the revisions of the German Temporary Employment Act, with an anticipated effective date of April 1, 2017. 6

This revision includes numerous changes with the primary purpose of avoiding the abuse of personnel leasing and the strengthening of leased personnel arrangements. 7

The essential new regulations will be (amongst others): 8

- Legal definition of personnel leasing;
- The maximum period of personnel leasing will be limited to 18 months;
- Equal pay needs to be guaranteed after nine months; in sectors with collective labor agreements for premiums (incremental increase of pay to core workers) equal pay must only be reached after 15 months;
- Ban of chain-, in-between- and continuous personnel lease (Ketten-, Zwischen- und Weiterverleih);
- Ban of using leased personnel for strike breaking;
- Temporary workers shall also be included in the headcount of the borrower.

With regards to international placement of personnel it remains unclear what the impact of the above changes will be. In particular the maximum of 18 months may cause difficulties as this would mean all international assignments to Germany are limited to a maximum of 18 months. However, it is expected that the privilege for assignments between affiliated companies will remain in place. 9

VI. Frequently Asked Questions about German Employment Law

1 In 2014 the publishers of this book published a book called German Employment Law – 618 Questions Frequently Asked by Foreigners.

The most relevant information to this text on expats and the corresponding questions are published here again. Please note that the numbers in this section have not been updated and reflect the situation from back when the first book was published.

Conclusion of an Employment Contract/Vertragsabschluss

Definition, Legal Principles:

2 As in most countries, an employment relationship in Germany is established with an employment contract. No employment contract law exists under German law. It is more the case that an employment contract is treated as a reciprocal relationship, as a subset of a service agreement under the German Civil Code. The employee obligates him/herself to performance and the employer to payment of a wage that has been agreed upon. Basically, an employment contract is based on the principle of freedom of contract. According to it, the parties can freely negotiate the content, signing and type of employment relationship. The limits of freedom of contract in Germany may be found in the principle of worker protection regulations, collective bargaining agreements, works agreements and case law.

Do contracts need to be concluded in writing?

3 No, a contract of employment of indefinite duration can be concluded orally and impliedly insofar as the law, collective bargaining agreement and works agreement do not stipulate otherwise. However, the employee has the right to have basic integral parts of the contract set in writing. These basic integral parts of the contract are:

- name and address of the contracting parties;
- start of the employment relationship;
- place of work;
- information about the work to be performed;
- compensation;
- notification periods and applicable collective bargaining agreements when appropriate;
- regarding a fixed term employment contract, the limited duration has to be in written form to be valid.

What applies if the prescribed written format is missing?

Employment contracts missing the prescribed form are valid and can be modified at any time with the consequence that subsequent agreements are legally valid, be they explicit or implicit. 4

Contrarily, agreements regarding collective bargaining agreements and works agreements are null and void if not in writing. 5

The missing prescribed form leads to an unfixed term employment for fixed-term contracts. 6

Can the contract also be drafted in a language other than German?

Yes, there is no legal obligation in Germany to draft or conclude an employment contract in the German language. Despite this fact, the language of the courts and relevant agencies in Germany is German, so the contract would have to be translated. Nowadays, more and more contracts are bilingually drafted. Should that be done one of those languages should be German, as that language is the chief one in Germany. 7

Does the employer have to draft the employment contract in the language of the foreign employee?

No, the translation of the contract into the language of a foreign employee is not required. On the other hand, the employment contract should be drafted in such a fashion that the employee can understand the basic integral parts of the contract. For the legal validity of the employment contract it suffices for the employee to have knowledge that the contract presented to him/her is their employment contract. If the employee has knowledge of this, the employer has fulfilled his duty to explain and consequently does not have to translate the contract or parts of it. In practice it is nevertheless commonplace in Germany to have the contract provided for in German and English in case of non-foreign workers. 8

Can an employment contract be signed by the parent or holding company?

The employment contract has to be signed by the contracting parties. Employment relationships do not exist with the corporation but instead with the individual company where the employee actually works. A holding company can only sign an employment contract as representative, but not as the primary employer. If the employer is not a subsidiary but instead the actual parent company, then the parent company should sign the contract. 9

Is there a minimum standard for contractual work conditions?

10 Yes, there is a law in Germany that lays out provisions to address such concerns, the so-called Act on Notification of Conditions Concerning the Employment Relationship (Nachweisgesetz – NachwG). Setting the fundamental contractual conditions in writing prevents ambiguities about the employment relationship and serves as evidence for the contracting partners in legal disputes. It represents a duty for the employer but not the validity of an employment contract that is only orally agreed upon.

Can there be fixed-term employment contracts in Germany?

11 Yes, and the German Act on Part-Time Work and Fixed-Term Employment sets the conditions.

What are the conditions of a limited-term contract?

12 The limited term of an employment relationship has to be justified by a factual reason provided there is no exception to the two-year term limitation. There is a factual reason in the following situations:

- the company needs are only temporary;
- the short-term is only due to the employee's training or schooling;
- the given position only exists because another employee is on leave;
- the particular nature of the job to be performed calls for it being temporary;
- the limited term serves as a test;
- the person of the employee can justify the limited term;
- the employee will be compensated by budgetary resources dedicated for the given job;
- cases of new companies or with new employees who have reached their 52nd birthday by the time they commence work.

Does the fixed term limitation have to be in writing?

13 The limited term of an employment contract needs to be in written form. An agreement about limiting the term that is not in writing represents a contract of employment that is of indefinite duration.

Are there special rules for start-up companies?

14 Newly founded companies can limit the employment contracts to which they agree to four years during their first four years of existence. The privilege can continue to have effect through to the end of the company's eighth year.

Can minors conclude a contract?

No, consent of a legal representative is required for the agreement's validity. Stipulations set out in the German Youth Employment Protection Act must be adhered to. So, for example, a child under age 15 represented by his/her legal guardian cannot conclude an employment contract. However, there are exceptions for internships and vacation jobs. 15

Does the works council need to take part in the concluding of contracts?

No, the works council has to be involved solely before the hiring. 16

Does the employer have a duty to disclose information?

This duty to explain or disclose information results from the relationship of reciprocal care between the employer and employee. The employer's duty in respect of care and supervision comes from a superior expertise or specialist's knowledge. In this respect, for example, the areas of company pension plans count here as long as it is based on an employer initiative. There will also be areas understood in this regard that are to be allocated to the employer's sphere (or responsibility), such as health risks and the avoidance of them. The employer has a duty to inform and explain the scope of the work to be performed and potential dangers at the workplace. 17

By what standard do employment contract clauses need to be measured?

Employment contract clauses have to be measured by legal standards. Clauses that represent a side agreement are subject to a content check. These clauses cannot be made in a fashion that works against the principles of good faith and thereby unreasonably disadvantage the employee. That is the case if the employee's rights become considerably restricted by such causes. Clauses that the employee would not normally have to expect are invalid. The German General Equal Treatment Act (Allgemeines Gleichbehandlungsgesetz – AGG) prohibits discrimination based on race, ethnicity, gender, religion or (secular) belief, disability of sexual identity and is thus also prohibited. Discriminatory practices are only permissible if it is vital requirement linked to the nature of the work. For example, it is permissible to limit midwife positions to females. 18

What data protection regulations need to be observed?

Regarding the employer's right to have the most comprehensive information possible about his/her employees, the employee has a right of self-determination regarding personal data. The usage of personal data is only permissible if it is legally provided or takes place with the consent of the affected person. Collection of personal 19 data is only allowed in an employment relationship if it is required for establishing, carrying out or ending an employment relationship. Prior consent is required, for example, in the context of an integration management program.

Can the content of a contract be governed by foreign law?

20 Yes, but the choice of legal system may not lead to the employee taking the compulsory protective measures of the country in which he/she works. The conclusion of an employment contract that accords with foreign law cannot, for example, work around German regulations regarding protections of unfair dismissal, maternity or of the severely handicapped.

When can an employment contract be contested?

21 An employment contract can be contested with the presentation of errors in content, declaration of intent or when there are mistakes about the characteristics of the document, or in cases of fraudulent misrepresentation. Contesting an employment contract due to fraudulent misrepresentation implies that the party accused of avoidance has lied about a matter of fact in an impermissible manner. If the employer asks the employee an impermissible question (i.e. regarding pregnancy) that employer is not entitled to appeal.

When is an employment contract void?

22 An employment contract is void when there is a violation of the law or bona mores, lacking legal capacity to contract or after an appeal.

Disciplinary Working/Abmahnung

Definition, Legal Principles

23 A disciplinary warning is a management tool. Legally, it is the precursor to a behavior-based regular dismissal or an extraordinary for cause. A disciplinary warning exists, then, if an employer points out a poor performance of work to an employee in a clear and recognizable manner. And, such a warning has to be given at a time which chronologically corresponds with the beach of contractual duties.

24 Through the disciplinary warning, the employee should be reminded of his/her contractual duties and warned about the consequences of further violations. For evidentiary purposes, the disciplinary warning should always be made in writing. If the employee is not in agreement with the disciplinary warning, he/she may go before a labor court to have the disciplinary warning removed from his/her personnel file.

What is a disciplinary warning understood to be in Germany?

A disciplinary warning is not regulated by law. It is understood as an employer's formal request to the employee to refrain from or perform a concretely denoted act when legal consequences are threatened. As in many other countries, it has the function of warning the employee. 25

What cannot be classified as a disciplinary warning?

No disciplinary warnings are 26
- co-worker suggestions;
- instructions;
- remonstrances;
- admonishments;
- reprimands.

Does an employer have to give disciplinary warnings?

The employer is only obligated to give disciplinary warnings if the employee has culpably carried out an infringement of contractual duties and for that reason the employer contemplates dismissal for reasons of conduct. The disciplinary warning and the repetition of the bad behavior is a prerequisite for the validity of dismissal as it supports to reason the perceived breach of contract. 27

How often can disciplinary warnings be issued?

Theoretically, the employer can issue a disciplinary warning for each instance of acting contrary to contract. Multiple written disciplinary warnings due to breaches of responsibility of the same kind for which no consequences result serve to weaken the effect of the warning so that termination of the employee is no longer possible despite further contractual violations. The employer should therefore assess how often he/she wishes to give disciplinary warnings prior to providing notice of dismissal. 28

Does a disciplinary warning have in written form?

No, a disciplinary warning may come in different forms. It can also come verbally. An exception exists when, for example, a collective agreement provides otherwise. For evidentiary purposes, the disciplinary warning must be given in writing. The description of the letter as disciplinary warning is not required. That said, a specific description is advisable for purposes of clarity. 29

What needs to be stated in the disciplinary warning?

30 The disciplinary warning has to concretely state the misconduct. General accusations are insufficient. Future behavior in accordance with the contract has to be formulated. The consequences in case of recurrence are also to be outlined. It suffices if it is made unmistakably clear that the employment relationship is endangered in case of a reoccurrence of the given violating act.

Who may issue a disciplinary warning?

31 The individual with the right to issue a disciplinary warning is someone who is authorized to discipline the affected person. Beyond the manager, immediate supervisors may be that person. The legal counsel authorized for this purpose is also entitled.

Who may not receive a disciplinary warning?

32 The individual tasked with data protection may not receive a disciplinary warning addressing his/her data protection duties. A member of the works council may not receive a disciplinary warning if the accusation of his acting contrary to contract relates to his work as a works council member.

What rights does the warned employee have?

33 That employee can have a counter-reply placed into his personnel file. Further, the employee can request the deletion or withdrawal of the disciplinary warning and have such action judicially enforced if the given warning is unjustified. The employee can immediately retract a disciplinary warning if it contains defamatory statements.

When is a disciplinary warning unjustified?

34 This is the case if one or more of the following applies:

- the disciplinary warning is not made in proper fashion that accords with regulations;
- it contains untrue statements of fact;
- it is based on erroneous assessment of employee behavior;
- the German principle of proportionality has been harmed, which, under German Employment Law, would mean that
- the employee has failed to make clear the rational relation between his/her means and the objective for the warning;
- the employer chose means that failed to keep the impairment of employee rights to a minimum;

- what is achieved was not proportional to the price with respect to infringement of rights;
- lastly, no defensible interest of the employer exists or the disciplinary warning contains generalized accusations.

What happens to the employer if a disciplinary warning is proven to be unjustified?
The disciplinary warning is to be removed from the personnel file. It cannot be used for notice of termination for reasons of conduct. In such a case, the dismissal would be invalid. 35

Dismissal/Arbeitgeber Kündigung

Definition, Legal Principles

Dismissal represents a one-sided ending of an employment relationship. What one must differentiate is immediate dismissal, or one for extraordinary circumstances without notice (außerordentliche), and ordinary (ordentliche) dismissal. An ordinary dismissal represents for both employer and employee the regular means of ending an employment relationship. On the other hand, an immediate dismissal is an exceptional means of ending employment relationships that have become unreasonable in nature and are for a discernibly important reason and, as a rule, is performed without notice. An immediate dismissal is uniformly regulated in sec. 626 of the German Civil Code for all types of employment relationships and is guaranteed as a constitutionally protected right to freedom for both contracting partners. For an ordinary dismissal that takes place within a set time period generally does not require grounds for the dismissal. That only applies, however, beyond the scope of the German Employment Protection Act (Kündigungsschutzgesetz). So long as the law finds application, reasons that rule out an unfair dismissal must exist. Then, the dismissal can only take place for operational reasons or on grounds of personal capability. The exact criteria for socially unjustified dismissals is defined by the German Labor Court. According to sec. 623 of the German Civil Code, all dismissals must be in writing. 36

General Aspects

Upon whom do the norms set out in the German Unfair Dismissal Act find application?
The German Unfair Dismissal Act finds application on those who work for operations that regularly have more than ten employees who are working for more than six months annually. For operations that have more than five employees, the Ger- 37

man Unfair Dismissal Act finds unlimited application only for those employees who began their employment relationship before January 1, 2004.

What notice periods apply under German law?

38 Notice periods in Germany are not uniformly regulated. They are found for example in the German Civil Code, special legal provisions, collective bargaining agreements, and in employment contracts. The statutory minimum notice period for employees who have completed their probationary period is four weeks. If the employer terminates the employee, the notice period depends on the length of the employment relationship and is between one and seven months. For the severely handicapped a notice period of four weeks is to be kept in mind. A collective bargaining agreement can lead to a variation in these notice periods.

What notice period applies for a probationary period?

39 German law prescribes a period of two weeks as a rule. Collective bargaining agreements often contain longer periods.

Can resignation from or termination of employment take place before the employment relationship begins?

40 Yes, the employee's resignation from a job or an employer terminating someone is possible before the employment relationship actually begins. According to German Federal Labor Court case law, the beginning of the notice period in which an employer must comply is based on the will of the parties. If there are shorter periods in the employment contract, the beginning of the notice period is presumed to begin upon receipt of notice and not when work actually commenced.

When does the employee have to receive notice?

41 Immediate dismissal for cause or extraordinary dismissal has to take place within two weeks after the party entitled to dismiss has acquired knowledge of the material facts for the dismissal. For an ordinary dismissal, such as one for poor performance, there is no statutorily defined deadline. The employer's right of termination is forfeited, however, if he/she delays on taking action for a longer time and thereby arouses legitimate confidence in the employee that the dismissal is not going to happen.

Can a short-term employment contract be canceled?

Based on legal principles, a short-term employment contract cannot be terminated. 42
There would need to be a clear statement in either an individual or collective bargaining agreement for that to happen.

Does termination have to be in writing? Is an e-mail or fax sufficient?

Yes, the termination of employment has to be in writing signed by hand or by way of 43
a notarially certified mark. A signed e-mail or fax does not suffice.

Who has to sign the termination letter?

The termination letter has to be hand-signed by the employer. As a rule, this is the 44
company's principal or its board of directors. Note: the principal (e.g. GM/CEO) may send an authorized representative but authorized representative should present a letter of authorization to dismiss employees. This is not required if the principal has informed the employee about the power of attorney being granted to a proxy, or the employee already has knowledge about the proxy. For this requirement it suffices if the proxy named in the commercial register signs in the manner prescribed there.

Where does the employee need to receive the notice?

The notice of termination can be given to the employee or an authorized third party, 45
be it at the workplace or mailed via postal service to the employee's residence. Delivery is considered to have taken place if the termination notice reaches a place where the recipient can reasonably anticipate it. In cases where it has been given to a third party or put into a mailbox, the notice of termination is considered delivered at the point when acknowledgement can be expected, e.g. the emptying of the mailbox.

When can employees not be terminated by notice?

Employees are not terminable by ordinary notice when they cannot be dismissed 46
using the same protocol that would be used for most employees. For example, works council members, youth and trainee representatives and severely handicapped may not be terminated by ordinary notice. Non-terminability can even be agreed upon in collective bargaining or individual agreements, by, for example, linking it to employment with the company.

The inability of being able to be terminated by notice does not preclude imme- 47
diate dismissal for cause. In individual cases, then, the ordinary termination process finds application in cases of immediate dismissal for cause.

Can the employer who is on vacation at the time be terminated?

48 Yes, absence due to the employee being on vacation does not preclude a notice of termination. Neither does it prevent the receipt of the notice of termination in the employee's absence.

Can the termination of employment be revoked by an employer?

49 No, as a unilateral declaration of intent that has to be received cannot revoke the legal force of received termination letter. The revocation of termination is to be seen as a request for a new employment relationship.

Extraordinary and Ordinary Dismissal

What types of notice are there?

50 A distinction is made between ordinary dismissal (ordentliche Kündigung) and immediate dismissal for cause (außerordentliche Kündigung).

What is an außerordentliche Kündigung?

51 Described in English, an außerordentliche Kündigung is a dismissal that terminates the contractual relationship for good cause without observing a notice period. Sometimes referred to in English as an extraordinary dismissal, it may only take place when taking into account both factors relevant to the circumstances of the particular case and the interests of both parties, and that the terminating party cannot be reasonably expected to continue working until the notice period expires or the agreed expiration of the contract; it is a dismissal that terminates the contractual relationship for good cause without observing a notice period.

Is there a time limit to keep for extraordinary dismissals?

52 Normally, a two-week notice period is the time limit applied, which means that the person giving notice only has two weeks after having securing knowledge of the facts that leads to the dismissal to declare the employment relationship terminated. Individual legal regulations and collective bargaining agreements can reduce this notice period even further.

What are the reasons for ordinary dismissal?

53 The German Unfair Dismissal Act (Kündigungsschutzgesetz) provides three reasons for a socially justified dismissal, the standard that must be met for an ordinary dismissal:

- operational reasons;
- behavioral reasons;
- those based on the person of the employee (i.e. the employee is unable to do the job).

Should the German Unfair Dismissal Act not apply, the dismissal has to be judged solely in accordance with the German principles of good faith (Treu und Glauben) and good morals (gute Sitten). 54

Do the reasons for dismissal need to be in the written notice?

Generally speaking, the reasons for the dismissal are not in a termination letter. As a result the employee sometimes does not know why he was dismissed. An exception would be cases of extraordinary dismissals, in which instance the employee can request a statement of reasons for termination; the missing information does not influence the validity of the dismissal but could lead to employee damage claims. It is indeed very rare that this might lead to compensation for damages. It could happen, however, in cases where the employee files a suit against the dismissal, loses the case and later claims that he/she would have not filed a claim if he/she had known the reasons. 55

Protection against Dismissal

What general protections of employees against dismissal exist in Germany?

For starters, the legislature only considers certain reasons of termination permissible. Employers have special requirements to observe depending on the grounds for termination. In cases of dismissal for operational reasons, the employer has a social selection procedure to carry out, and must explain the business decisions that lead to the elimination of positions. A warning is required as part of a termination for behavioral reasons. In cases of termination for reasons related to the person of the employee, the employer has to do everything within his/her power to avoid terminating the given employment relationship. 56

What special protections of employees against dismissal exist in Germany?

Special protections against dismissal appear in the protections of certain groups of people. These groups enjoy protection from ordinary. 57

What applies for pregnant women?

58 The agreement of the body authorized according to state law (Landesrecht) has to be asked for approval before dismissing a pregnant employee. This depends on the state or regional governments or regional council. A dismissal carried out without the necessary approval is invalid and cannot be remedied.

Can a severely handicapped employee be terminated?

59 Yes, a severely handicapped person's employment relationship can be terminated. That said, severely handicapped persons working in Germany enjoy a special protection against unfair dismissal. This stipulates special requirements regarding the type of dismissal, such as obtaining the approval of the German Integration Offices (Integrationsamt) for the dismissal. One carried out without the necessary approval is invalid and cannot be remedied.

Can a works council member have his/her employment terminated?

60 Works Council members enjoy a special protection from unfair dismissal. The ordinary dismissal of a works council member is not possible. Indeed works council members can only be terminated by extraordinary means, which means that the employer has to demonstrate that continuing the employment relationship is unreasonable.

Can the employer fire an employee because he/she is unable to work due to illness?

61 Yes, dismissal due to an illness preventing the ability to work represents a dismissal for reasons related to the person of the employee. It only comes into question if the illness seriously impacts the employment relationship. This may be the case if the performance of work is not possible for a longer time (1.5 years) or if the duration of the inability to work due to illness is principally short but recurrent. Plainly stated, the employer is not be expected to wait indefinitely for the recovery of the employee (principle of proportionality). What is decisive here is the requirement of having a clearly negative prognosis for the development of the employee according to objective standards. The point in time of the dismissal is decisive for the prognosis.

Can an older employee be dismissed because he/she works more slowly than his/her co-workers?

62 Firing a so-called "low performer" is only possible under the strictest conditions. The most important point here is what work the employer can fairly expect. With older employees it is common that their work performance diminishes. Dismissal of

the employee for such reasons would be seen as being in violation of the principles of social considerations stipulated by German labor law.

Obligations of the Employer in case of Dismissal

Does the employer have to provide a letter of reference?

Yes, the employer is obligated to provide a reference letter. 63

Which documents does the employer have to provide in case of dismissal?

The employer has to provide an interim reference letter for the application process, 64
as well as a final reference letter on the employee's work. Due to a secondary obligation derived from German Employment Law, the employer must also provide a statement of income.

The employer has to demonstrate all of the facts that could be considered with 65
respect to the decision about a claim to unemployment pay or a transitional allowance by the time employment has been concluded. Further, the employer has to provide the employee with a report of the given calendar year's used and remaining vacation time.

Does the employer have to give the employee a disciplinary warning before giving notice of dismissal?

An advanced disciplinary warning is required in scope of dismissal for behavior in 66
ordinary conditions. The requirement of a disciplinary warning results from the prevailing principle of proportionality found in the German Unfair Dismissal Act. A dismissal should be the last resort (principle of ultima ratio). The employer has to inform the employee of his/her wrongdoing (Rüge, or written reprimand) and through this afford him/her the chance to act in a manner conforming to the contract in the future (Ermahnung, or verbal caution). Secondly, the employer has to make the employee aware that his job is in danger if he repeats the given behavior (Warnung, or warning). There is no obligation to warn if the employer cannot achieve his/her intended aims with warnings (i.e. written reprimand, verbal caution, warning).

Involvement of the Works Council and the Boards of Directors

Does the works council or union have to be heard regarding a dismissal?

If the company has a works council, the given works council has to be informed be- 67
fore the notification of dismissal is made. Union input is not required for a dismissal.

Can the employer dismiss an employee if the works council objects?

68 It is true that the objection of the works council does not prevent an employer from dismissing an employee. However, a works council objection for an ordinary dismissal provides the right to continued employment with the employer until a legally binding conclusion of the legal dispute.

What applies to dismissal during the probationary period?

69 The company also has to inform the works council before notifying an employee of termination during the probationary period.

Does the board of directors have to be heard regarding a dismissal?

70 The board of directors does not have to be heard regarding a dismissal. Occasional personnel measures by executives can require the approval of the board of directors.

En Masse Layoffs

What does the employee need to keep in mind if a large number of employees are going to be laid off (en masse layoffs, or Massenentlassung)?

71 In cases of en masse layoffs, the employer has an obligation to notify of and receive consultation on the decision. The employer has to report the en masse layoff to the German Federal Employment Agency and the works council and share with the works council information about the layoff plans. In Germany, a mass layoff is considered en masse if an employer with 21 to 59 employees wishes to lay off five of them, with 60 to 499 wishes to lay off 10%, or one with at least 500 employees wishes to lay off at least 30 employees.

If an employer is laying people off, does that employer have to release employees from having to work in order to search for a job?

72 There is an obligation under German law to release employees to search for another job if the release from having to work takes place in what the employer considers a reasonable scope with an ongoing payment obligation. However, employees have the right to continue their work until termination date. The employer cannot release them from their duty of works without valid reasons.

Legal Action against Dismissal

What happens if the employee files a complaint regarding his/her dismissal?

Legal action for dismissal allows the person dismissed the possibility of invalidating the dismissal. If the person dismissed does not assert a claim before the German Labor Court within three weeks after having received the termination letter that the employment relationship has not been terminated by the given notice of termination, the notice of termination is considered legally effective from the outset. 73

Can documents that are not in German language be provided to the German courts?

No, the judicial language is German. Submitting documents that are not in German is legally insufficient. They have to be translated. 74

Employee Liability/Arbeitnehmerhaftung

Definition, Legal Principles

Employee liability deals with whether or, if, then in what scope the employee can be made responsible for damages that occurred in the course of carrying out his/her work. If the work-related accident involves damage to persons, the right to statutory accident insurance comes into play (German Social Security Code (SGB, Art. VII). For all other damages the authority of principles developed by case law on internal compensatory damages apply. 75

What is meant with employee liability in Germany?

The term employee liability deals with the scope and under what conditions the employee has to compensate the employer for damages the employee caused in the process of carrying out his/her work in a non-compliant fashion. 76

For what is the employee liable to the employer?

The scope of the liability is based on the degree of the blame. In cases of minor negligence – thus, less attributable blame – the employee is not liable (e.g. in cases of typical going astray ("typischen Abirrens"): offending someone else, ("Sich-Vergreifen"), misspeaking ("Sich-Versprechen") or making a mistake ("Sich-Vertun"), German Federal Labor Court (BAG), Urt. v 28.10.2010 – 8 AZR 418/09). In cases of moderate negligence – thus, moderate attributable blame – the employee has proportionate liability. In order to calculate the loss ratio, then totality of the circumstances of the given situation (amount of damages, predisposition to/risk of danger, 77 etc.) what to factor in (e.g. with damages to a company vehicle, it is of significance whether the employer has full comprehensive insurance. He/she is not obligated, therefore the non-conclusion of analysis at the expense of the employer in the given situation can be of considerable importance; the employee is only liable for the deductible, which would have been negotiable upon signing a comprehensive insurance agreement). In gross negligence cases, employee liability is unlimited unless he/she is deemed worthy of (legal) protection (schutzwürdig) (e.g. forgetting an unsecured briefcase at a restaurant, driving under the influence of alcohol, driving through a red light). If the employee is handled in accordance with rules and regulations, he has unlimited liability.

How is the risk of liability shared between employer and employee?

78 Risk of liability is shared between employer and employee. A proportion is normally determined by mutual agreement of the employer and employee; courts decide in cases of dispute. How high the employee's portion is depends on the circumstances of the particular situation. That means that German law gives consideration of circumstances that work in favor of and against the employee, e.g. past actions, type and difficulty of the task, level of damage, risk of damage.

Can there be a limit to liability for the employee?

79 Only in exceptional cases can there be a limit to liability. It is the case if the employee's earnings are in clear disproportion to the liability risk of the task. Only in exceptional cases can there be a limit to liability. It is the case if the employee's earnings are in clear disproportion to the liability risk of the task. The limitation of liability with gross negligence will not be precluded by the German Federal Labor Court in these cases. Whether and to what extent the loss ratio appears justified, is to be judged in respect to the violation of obligation and the amount of damages. The German Federal Labor Court has not imposed a loss ratio that exceeds the annual income of the affected person. For example: 4 months' salary in an automobile accident, 12 months' salary for a minijob.

Illness/Krankheit

Definition, Legal Principles

80 When ill employees are entitled to continued remuneration for up to six months according to German law. Collective bargaining agreements can deviate from this and provide for a longer time. The average number of days lost due to illness for 2012 by those in the state health care system was 3.64%. This works out to about 14 days missed. There has been a noticeable increase in sick days taken over the last few

years. Illness-related days taken should be reported to the employer without delay, not least those taken due to work environment and trust.

Does the employee have to the notify the employer of his/her illness?

German law mandates that employees who are ill have to notify the employer of illness without undue delay. A telephone call suffices to serve this end so long as nothing to the contrary has been agreed upon by the two parties. If the illness causes an inability to work for more than three days, the employee has to provide the employer with a doctor's note or certificate of inability to work by no later than the fourth day the employee is out due to illness. However, the employer may request a certificate of inability to work as early as the first day out of the office. This right of the employer is not within the unbound discretion of the employer. It is not especially necessary, for example, that there is an accusation against the employee that he/she has previously only faked an illness. **81**

What is a certificate of inability to work (Arbeitsunfähigkeitsbescheinigung)?

The German "certificate of inability to work" is more than a sick note; it is a certificate from a licensed physician that names the person and provides the length of time that person will be out ill and unable to work. **82**

What applies to foreign certificates of inability to work?

Foreign certificates of this nature principally have come to possess the same evidentiary value as a domestic certificate of inability to work. What is required is that the foreign certificate is actually a certificate of inability to work and is not a mere sick note. **83**

Does the employee have to tell the employer about the precise illness?

Generally not. Such a notification requirement exists only if the employer has a justifiable reason to know what the diagnosis is. An example of such a justification would be when the cause for one person being unable to work becomes an issue where the employer has to take safety measures to protect other employees, has influence on the obligation to continue paying wages or because someone else has been injured by it. **84**

Does the employer have to pay the employee if he is ill?

Yes, the employer is obligated to continue paying wages for the first six weeks of the employee's inability to work. Afterward the health insurance and state social secu- **85** rity comes into effect. Alone the burden of continuing to pay the employee does not entitle the employer to give the employee notice of termination due to illness.

What rules apply to long-term illnesses?

86 An illness is long-term if the employee is rendered unable to work at the capacity he/she is expected to as a result of the illness. To meet this standard, the employee's inability to work has to be for a period of approximately 1.5 years.

87 A long-term illness may justify an ordinary dismissal so long as the recovery cannot be projected. However, this is a rare case in Germany.

What applies to repeated illness(es)?

88 What is decisive here is whether the inability to work is based on a new illness or the same one. If the repeated inability to work is based on another illness, the employee has an unrestricted entitlement to continued compensation.

89 On the other hand, if the same illness is the cause of the inability to work, the employer only has an obligation to continue to pay wages if the time missed due to the same illness does not exceed six weeks within no more than a six-month period. The employer still has to continue to pay wages as well if twelve months elapse between the first incidence of the employee's inability to work and the new period during of his/her inability to work.

Can the employer have the employee commit to preventative medical care or rehabilitation measures?

90 No, but different rules may apply to certain business sectors and particular jobs. In those sectors, a medical check-up can be set as a mandatory condition for service, such as for pilots.

Does the employer have to cover the costs for the employee's treatment?

91 No, the payer are of preventative medical care and rehabilitation measures:
- the German Federal Employment Agency;
- Health Insurers;
- accident or worker's compensation insurance;
- war victim assistance carriers;
- public-sector youth worker welfare carriers;
- the statutory health insurance system.

Does the employer have to take precautionary measures, e.g. vaccinations, training to minimize back pain, eye exams, provide a company gym, dietary counseling, etc.?

Beyond the usual facilities and furnishings of the workplace, no requirement of the 92
employer to provide precautionary measures exist. However, if the employee is declared to be unable to work for more than six weeks within a one-year period, the employer is obligated to attempt preventing the employer from getting a renewed illness of the same sort (e.g. by improving the work environment).

What happens if the employee had a work-related accident?

If an accident takes place on the premises of the workplace, a company-approved 93
physician must be consulted. The chosen physician has to have been approved by the trade association, specializing in work and commuting-related accidents. Further, the employer and the physician performing treatment has to report the accident to the employer's liability insurance company using a special form.

What happens if the employee gets into an accident on the way to or from work that prevents that makes that employee unable to work?

A workplace accident is a situation for the statutorily mandated accident insurance. 94
It is to be differentiated from pure free-time activities, sports and non-work-related driving accidents (insured activities). If the employee is injured on his way from home to his/her workplace, he/she is insured. Such injuries are defined as being ones that take place on the way to or from the workplace (Wegeunfälle). They are a sub-form of workplace accidents. They are conditioned on an interrelationship between the insured activity and the distance covered. It is of influence to insurance coverage that the injured person took the most direct route. Of immediate importance in such a case is that the injured person freely chose the shortest time in time or distance, as well as which mode of transportation was to be used. Should the injured person have, for example, taken an alternate route/short cut, the injury is not covered by insurance unless it is of minimal significance. There are therefore alternate routes expressly permitted by law; e.g. picking up a carpool participant or transporting children to a daycare or childcare giver.

What happens if a third party caused the accident leading to the employee's inability to work?

If a third party caused an employee's inability to work, the injured employee has a 95
right to collect damages from that third party who cased it. This claim to damages includes reimbursement for lost wages. Since the employer is obligated to continue paying wages for a six-week period, German law provides that there be no loss of

wages for the employee who is rendered unable to work. The employee's claim against the liable party (tortfeasor) is transferred in this respect to the employer. The employee is obligated to furnish the given employer with the information required to assert these rights.

May the employee pursue secondary employment during the time he/she is out?

96 No, the employee may not pursue secondary employment during the time which he/she is out because of illness or injury so long as it can harm the process or healing or getting better. If the employee violates this rule, he/she may be reprimanded (see: "Chapter 6: Disciplinary Working/Abmahnung").

May the employee do yard work, gardening, or sports during the time he/she is out?

97 The employee has to commit him/herself to "health-enhancing" behavior. Whether the employee's behavior is enhancing health or not must be determined on a case-by-case basis, as everyone is different. In certain cases, as with mental illnesses, for example, gardening can be seen as promoting health and would therefore be permitted. But, if the employee has a flu-like illness which renders him/her bed-ridden, gardening would, of course, be forbidden.

Part Time/Teilzeit

Definition, Legal Principles

98 While the number of full-time employees in Germany has been decreasing, the number of part-timers has been steadily increasing. Every employee has a right to reduce or redistribute working hours according to sec 8 of the Part-time Work and Fixed-term Employment Contracts Act (Teilzeit- und Befristungsgesetz). To begin, part-time employees cannot be treated worse than their full-time counterparts. For this reason, additional benefits such as Christmas bonuses have to be proportionally paid out to part-timers as well.

Are full-time employees entitled to a work part-time hours?

99 Yes, but a requirement for this is that the employee has been working for the given employer for at least six months. Additionally, a request for part-time work can only be made biennially.

What has to be in an application for part-time work?

A general requirement is that the request be formulated in a way that allows the employer to reply with a simple "yes". What the request has to make very clear is that the employee wishes to work reduced working hours and the scope of those hours. 100

Does the request need to be made in writing?

No, as the law makes no such requirement. The request should nevertheless be put in writing in order to provide a paper trail should one be needed. 101

When can the employer refuse part-time work?

If the employer does not wish to approve the request for part-time work, he/she has to be able to counter with rational, imaginable operational reason. As a rule, there are sufficiently serious grounds to deny part-time work if the reduced working hours considerably impair the organization, work flow or security in the workplace, or bring about disproportionate costs. 102

How far in advance does the employee have to submit his/her part-time work request?

This has to be done at least three months prior to when the employee wishes to invoke his/her right to working part-time. 103

When does the employer have to decide on a part-time work request?

The employer has to inform the employee about whether the requested period for part-time work has been agreed to no later than one month before that time period commences. Should the employer fail to do this, the working times the employee requested will be granted automatically. 104

Does every company have to allow for part-time hours?

No. The right to part-time exists only if the employer employs at least 15 employees. 105

How are the 15 employees counted?

All employees who regularly work for the given employer are to be counted, regardless of the number of hours the employee works. Trainees are not counted. Temporary employees are to be counted if they work regularly for the employer. Basically, a per capita principle is applied so that even marginally employed persons are counted. 106

What happens if the employer denies the request for part-time work?

107 In such a case, the employee would have the right to take his case to court. What comes into consideration is an action for performance, namely, the consent to change an existing employment contract. However, this does not entitle the employee to be absent from work.

What points should definitely be stipulated in a part-time employment agreement?

108 The following should definitely be stipulated: weekly working times/days, the concrete work obligations, compensation, vacation time, the proportionate workload reduction, probationary period, confidentiality obligations, company rules and collective wage agreements, the saving clause (a clause that, among other things, provides that the rest of an agreement will not become invalid if one part does).

Is the general entitlement to part-time the only means for reducing working hours?

109 No, since, beyond the general entitlement to part-time work, there are also special legal provisions granting a decrease in working hours for certain employees. These groups include parents during the duration of their parental leave or employees who have to look after relatives in need of nursing care.

Is there a right to part-time work after the conclusion of agreed upon parental leave ends?

110 In principle, the employment relationship is revived after parental leave ends. This depends on if the parent in question had worked part-time during the parental leave or not. Accordingly, employees can assert a right to working part-time after their parental leave ends.

After parental leave ends, does the employee have to be back to work full-time again for six months before he/she can request part-time hours from the employer?

111 If the employment relationship has existed already for six months, the employee can submit a request to work part-time work after parental leave has ended. Parental leave is calculated as time employed, since the employment relationship continued during this period. What one must watch out for is that he/she adheres to the three-month deadline for submitting the timeframe for part-time work.

How is the vacation time of part-timers calculated?

112 The problem with calculating vacation time often arises if flexible work hours were agreed to and the range of hours per day worked varies. Here, the first thing to be

calculated is how many days the employee works at the company on average. The nominal amount of vacation days for a full-time employee, multiplied by the actual number of days worked by an employee working part-time during a specific number of working days that set the base period, divided by the number of working days for a full-time employee during the set base period.

How does part-time employment end?

It can end in one of two ways: termination of employment or a change in contract. 113
With termination of the employment relationship, through a severance agreement, it can be ended with notice or via the conclusion of a valid fixed-term. Further, part-time work can be ended with mutually agree upon change to the contract.

Does an employee have a right to return to full-time work after a having worked reduced hours?

As a rule, there is no right for an employee to return to the same job after having 114
worked in a part-time capacity. However, all employees working part-time who wish to extend their working hours do indeed have a right to be considered preferentially by employers for full-time positions indeed.

Pregnancy/Parental Leave/Schwangerschaft/Elternzeit

Definition, Legal Principles

In 2011, approximately 663,000 children were born in Germany, with a large num- 115
ber of mothers working in addition to fathers. The spirit of German laws on the matter hold that the employment relationship of pregnant woman and their unborn children should be protected from workplace dangers during the pregnancy by the provisions of extant maternity laws. Further, legal principles are the prescription of occupational health and safety regulations for the protection of mothers (MuSchArbV). Generally, these protections apply to all pregnant women, even those in mini-jobs, working out of the home, or in trainee- or apprenticeships. There is also the possibility of taking parental leave after the birth of the child, the longest period being through the end of the child's third year of life. By way of parental leave, parents should be given the chance to dedicate time their time to raising and caring for their child without the fear of their employment relationship being terminated by their respective employer.

General Aspects

What is the difference between pregnancy leave and parental leave?

116 Pregnancy describes, of course, the period during which a mother carries a baby to term. However, parental leave begins with the birth of the child.

117 Parental leave has the purpose of making the care for and rearing of a child easier for working parents and guardians. During the term of the parental leave, the employer releases the employee from having to perform the work the employee does.

118 Expecting mothers can choose whether or not to work during the six weeks leading up to the birth of their child. However, mothers are strictly prohibited from working in the eight weeks after their baby's birth. This is a right mothers cannot waive.

Pregnancy

Do are there prohibitions on working and under what conditions?

119 Expecting mothers may not work in the six weeks prior to their child's birth unless she clearly states her intent to work. Beyond this, expecting mothers may not work if the job being performed has detrimental effects, e.g. radiation or substances that could harm her health or subject her to harmful vapors of gases. Further, expecting mothers may not perform:

- extra work/overtime;
- night shifts;
- work on weekends or holidays.

120 Lastly, mothers are strictly prohibited from working in the first eight weeks after their baby's birth.

From what point in time can a mother return to work?

121 A mother may not work until eight weeks post-partem. During the eight-week period post-partem, mothers are strictly prohibited from working in Germany. In individual cases where a woman either gives birth to multiple children or prematurely delivers a child, the period of legal protection is extended to twelve weeks after delivery of the child or children. In order for a premature birth to be medically determined to be as such, a medical certificate testifying to this fact is required. Should the child weigh under 2500 grams or the child if he/she has not reached the necessary signs of maturity set by qualified medical professionals, the child is considered by German law to be premature. If the child was born exceptionally early, the legal protection may be extended even further and would be increased by the precise amount of time the baby was born early.

Can a pregnant woman be dismissed from her job?

No, a pregnant woman may not be dismissed from her job for up to four months post partem. That said, her employer has to know about the pregnancy, or be made aware no later than two weeks following receipt of her termination notice. 122

Motherhood Allowance

What is the so-called motherhood allowance (Mutterschaftsgeld)?

Motherhood allowance is a subsidy. It is paid during the phase when the mother is under maternity protection. In Germany, that means six weeks prior to and eight weeks after birth of the child. 123

Does an entitlement to motherhood allowance exist?

An entitlement exists only if the woman has a fixed employment relationship with the employer. This also includes women who are working out of the home. Additionally, the woman has to have statutory health care coverage. Otherwise, when she is insured privately, the woman receives a one-time motherhood allowance payment. 124

Parental Leave

Who is entitled to parental leave?

Employees who are entitled to parental leave include those, be they male or female, who have a working relationship with the given employer at the time of applying for this leave, and this includes those employees completing vocational training, part-time employees, temporary employees, students doing side jobs and those working from home and those in equivalent employment relationships. Others who have a right to parental leave are adoptive parents, foster parents, or relatives of the child. The former have rights similar to the biological parents; the latter have these rights only in special cases. 125

Can someone be barred from his/her right to parental leave entitlement?

No, the entitlement to parental leave is mandatory statutory law. It cannot be barred by contract or limited. 126

Work agreements and collective bargaining agreements that affect the employment status of the employee before or after the parental leave are illegal. With the presentation of qualifying criteria for the entitlement, the employer cannot legally prevent an employee from taking parental leave. 127

Are there special rules regarding adopted and foster children?

128 Yes, parental leave can be taken for adopted and foster children for a three-year period beginning at the time the child is officially taken into the employee's home. It ends once the child reaches his/her eighth birthday.

Does there need to be a written contract about parental leave?

129 An explanation of the usage is required. Regarding content, German law requires that the employee requests parental leave and, at the same time, communicates the specific dates for the beginning and end of the time to be taken, taking the parental leave within two years. The employee has to request parental leave in writing and the employer has to certify it.

What happens to the employment relationship with the employer during parental leave?

130 The employment relationship continues, but the primary job obligations are suspended for the duration of the parental leave.

Can someone on parental leave be dismissed from a job?

131 In Germany, there is a special protection against unfair dismissal. This special protection is valid from the point in time when parental leave that is in line with procedures and deadlines is requested. The protection exists during the parental leave and no more than eight weeks before the start of that leave. During the time special protection against unfair dismissal is valid, the employer may not terminate the employment relationship he/she has with the employee. Only in exceptional cases can the highest state-level office responsible for employment protection matters or a authority it has designated declare such a termination permissible.

May the employer mandate parental leave?

132 No, the claim to parental leave depends entirely on the initiative of the employee. So, if the employee does not request parental leave, the employer cannot, for example, thereby counteract an existing overstaffing issue by way of his/her authority to give directions in a given situation.

Are there particular deadlines to observe?

133 Yes, the notification period to make the claim is usually seven weeks. A shorter time limit is only possible if urgent reasons prevent adherence to the standard period.

For how long can someone go on parental leave?

According to German law, an employee may take parental leave until the child's 134 third birthday. The time of the maternity protection period is to be deducted from that, which is counted against the time allotted. Parental leave ends with the end of the child's third year of life. In other words, the employee has to return to work by the child's third birthday. So long as the employer agrees, up to a twelve-month portion of parental leave can be taken at a later time, and that time must be before the child's eighth birthday.

How much parental leave is there if there are fewer than three years between the birth of other children?

In cases of multiple children, parents are entitled to three years of parental leave for 135 each child, even if the three-year-time limit alluded to in the German Law on Parental Allowance and Parental Leave (Gesetz zum Elterngeld und zur Elternzeit – BEEG) has been exceeded.

Can parental leave be broken up into different time periods?

Yes, parental leave can be split into two time periods; breaking the leave down into 136 more time periods requires the agreement of the employer.

Can parental leave be extended?

The initially intended time period can be extended by mutual agreement. Thus, the 137 consent of the employer is required. The employer therefore possesses the right to reject an extension of parental leave until it verges on abuse of the right and may be construed as harassment.

Can parental leave be ended early?

Shortening the declared time of parental leave is only permissible with the consent 138 of the employer. Otherwise the ability of the employer to rely on his business planning is endangered. Thus, the consent is at the discretion of the employer. Other rules apply in more difficult situations, such as cases of a child's premature death.

Does illness prior to the planned start of parental leave have an effect on the ability to take the leave?

No, as the parties involved will have already made a binding agreement. The same 139 applies when the parental leave ends. Even if the employee is ill to this point, parental leave ends as agreed upon.

Are parents on parental leave entitled to vacation time?

140 Yes, but not in its entirety. Employers are entitled to reduce the vacation time the employee has for a given year by one-twelfth for each month of the parental leave. However, if the employee works part-time during the parental leave, the employer does not have a right to reduce the employee's vacation time.

May an employee work elsewhere during parental leave?

141 Yes, but the employee needs the employer's consent in order take on another employment. To this end, there must be an application made in which the specific type and amount of time for the alternative work is communicated to the employer. Furthermore, the other employer has to be named in the application.

Parental-leave Allowance

What is parental-leave allowance (Elterngeld)?

142 Parental-leave allowance is a governmental social benefit and subsidy for families.

Who is entitled to the parental-leave allowance?

143 A cut-off date regulation applies with respect to the parental-leave allowance. That means that parents whose child was born on or after January 1, 2007 receive the benefit. The parent entitled to an income replacement benefit is the one who stops working after the child's birth in order to care for the child.

How much can the parental-leave allowance be?

144 Mothers or fathers will receive monthly payments of 67% of their last net income (on average, twelve months before the child's birth); the cap is 1,800 € per month.

How long is parental-leave allowance paid out?

145 Parental-leave allowance is limited to twelve months. It can, however, be extended to 14 months if both partners stop working. The so-called "partner months" can be freely divided during those two extra months.

Who can apply for parental-leave allowance?

146 Parental-leave allowance has to be applied for at the office responsible for education allowances (Erziehungsgeldstelle); depending on where you live in Germany, it is either the youth or social welfare office.

Part-time Work during Parental Leave

Does the employer have to offer a part-time position to parents who are taking parental leave?

The German Law on Parental Allowance and Parental Leave provides for the possibility of working part-time during parental leave. Accordingly, employees – male or female – are entitled to working part-time for the duration of their parental leave. However, the right to part-time work in accordance with the German Law on Parental Allowance and Parental Leave is different than the one under the Act on Part-Time and Fixed-Term Employment (Teilzeitvorschriften des Teilzeit- und Befristungsgesetzes – TzBfG). One considerable difference between Part-time Work and Fixed-term Employment Contracts Act and the Parental Allowance and Parental Leave rights to working part-time is that the latter right is only protected for the duration of the parental leave. However, the part-time work entitlement according to the Part-time Work and Fixed-term Employment Contracts Act changes the scope of contractually required working time for perpetuity. At the end of the parental leave, the employee is again contractually obliged to work without a need for an explicit agreement by the contracting parties. 147

What information needs to be in the application to work part-time?

An application for part-time work during parental leave has to lay out the start and scope of the shortened work day. The employee can give the desired break down of the shortened work day. 148

Reference (from Employers)/Zeugnis

Definition, Legal Principles

In Germany employees have a right to a written reference at the end of the employment relationship. The legal basis may be found in sec. 109 of the German Industrial Code (Gewerbeordnung – GewO), which applies uniformly to all employees in Germany. 149

For trainees and apprentices, the right to a reference is controlled by the German Vocational Act (Bundesbildungsgesetz – BBiG). Above all, an employee reference serves the employee's further professional development. The reference makes enables the employee to prove his/her job history and personal and professional capabilities. Additionally, the reference helps future employers in the process of selecting new employees. 150

In the one hand, the reference must conform to the truth; on the other hand, it should reflect the good will of the employer. Due to the tension between good will and obligation to tell the truth, it is not uncommon that disputes over the contents of refer- 151 ences come before labor courts. The reason may be the well-known "secret code" of references: what seems to be a positively worded characteristic can have a certain touch or hint that can lead one to draw a negative conclusion. In exceptional, justifiable cases (e.g. change in supervisor) an interim performance review is also justified.

Is every employee entitled to an employer reference letter?

152 Yes, in Germany, every employee has a right to a reference from his/her employer.

What function does this reference serve?

153 The reference serves the professional advancement of the employee. It also gives employers who are looking for staff-selection criteria for filling positions.

When does the reference have to be issued by the employer?

154 The employer owes the employee the reference at the end of the employment relationship. A general letter of reference has to be produced without the urging of the employee. A "qualifiziertes Zeugnis" – a reference detailing the qualifications of the employee (e.g. supervisory roles, accomplishments, etc.) – is to be issued if the employee expresses that he/she needs one.

What is in a basic reference (einfaches Zeugnis)?

155 The type of work and length of time worked by the employee are to be denoted.

What is in a "qualifiziertes Zeugnis"?

156 As suggested earlier, the term "qualified" is not negatively applied here; a German "qualified" reference from the employer has to include all important facts about and assessments of the employee that would be of interest and significance to future employers. For example, information about the performance and conduct of the employee are to be indicated. Note: The evaluation of job performance has to be based on the job description. The employee's conduct addresses the social behavior between him/her and superiors, co-workers and others in the workplace.

What are Bescheinigungen?

157 As compared to the Zeugnis, or reference from the employer, the Bescheinigungen are certificates that represent evidence of the nature of the employment with third parties. In Germany, a Zeugnis is generally understood to mean one which is "qualified", one that indicates the accomplishments and positive aspects of the em-

ployee's person and work. The common understanding of einfaches Zeugnis is that of a mere certificate indicating employment.

What is the general content needed for a reference from the given employer?

The content is determined by how the purpose of supporting the employee's profes- 158
sional advancement can best be served. That means the appearance, choice of words, date created and who signs it have to correspond with the normal customs of business operations.

How should a typical German reference from an employer look (e.g. handwritten, what paper, etc.)?

A reference should be typed and on the company letterhead that is used in regular 159
business; on that paper the full address and company name, legal form (e.g. Inc., GmbH, etc.) and the current address are to be listed.

What employee HR information has to be included in the reference from the employer?

The precise and full first and last name of the employee, and, where appropriate, 160
date of birth are to be indicated. The date of birth is only to be included with employee consent.

Does a reference from the employer have to show the reference's issue date?

Yes, and the reference's issue date and the date of its actual creation are usually the 161
same.

By whom does the reference from the employer have to be signed?

A reference from the employer is finalized when signed by the employer by hand or 162
its negotiating representative. Facsimiles, photocopied signatures, e-mails or faxes are insufficient.

Does the reference from the employer have to include employee health information?

No, employee health information does not belong in a reference from the employer. 163

Does the employee's membership in the works council or trade union involve- 164
ment have to be included?

No, that would only be included at the request of the employee.

Is it common in Germany to include a grade for the employee in the reference from the employer?

165 Giving a grade to the employee is not required, but it is common to evaluate the employee's work with a grade (they would be as follows: 1 = A; 1- = A-; 2+ = B+; 2 = B; 2- = B-, etc.).

Does the reference from the employer have to include the reason why the employee is leaving?

166 Only if the employee wishes to have the reason for leaving included in the reference should it be included.

Does the employer make him/herself liable for damages if he/she fails to provide the employee with a reference?

167 Yes, the employee could find the employer culpable for damages for a delayed reference from that employer, if the letter is incorrect, or if the employer fails to even produce one. The damages due consists of the loss of income that the employee suffers by not getting the position applied for due to the current employer's delayed, incorrect or missing reference.

Typical Employment Contract Content/Typische Arbeitsvertragsinhalte

Definition, Legal Principles

168 Employer and employee can principally form the terms of the contract freely. The German Law on Notification of Conditions Governing an Employment Relationship (Nachweisgesetz) provides a guide to what minimum content legislators have stipulated and will want to have put into writing. This includes, for example, names of the employment contract partners, workplace location, scope and amount of vacation time as well as the amount and definition of duties to be performed. Beyond these basic rules are the practical questions of interest, such as those regarding employer loans, making company property available, usage of company automobiles, etc. Here, contractual partners can negotiate freely so long as no valid works or collective bargaining agreement states otherwise.

Does the employer have to make a PC, mobile phone, and the like available to the employee?

169 The employer is obligated to make available all work and occupational safety equipment necessary for the employee to carry out the job required of him/her. This includes office supplies.

Does the employer have to allow the private usage of PCs, mobile devices, and the like?

No, this is not required. Different regulations apply if such consent is provided in an individual employment contract or collective bargaining agreement. 170

Does the employer have to pay for length-of-service bonuses or employee participation programs?

No, as no such obligation exists. Different rules apply if such payments are allowed by an individual employment contract or a collective bargaining agreement. A claim to payment of an anniversary bonus exists when a company norm is established through repeated payments of this sort. 171

May the employee pursue secondary employment?

Yes, so long as the employment relationship with the primary employer is not impaired and the legal cap on hours worked daily does not exceed ten hours. The employer can only prohibit an employee from taking on secondary employment for legitimate interests and then refuses to grant the consent required. A recognized legitimate interest for the employer is work at a rival company. 172

Does the employer have to grant employee loans?

No, the employer does not. However, different rules apply if they are provided for by an individual employment contract or a collective bargaining agreement, something which is uncommon. 173

May employees take on roles of honorary office?

Yes, so long as the role does not prevent or make entirely impossible the completion of his/her normal work. 174

May an employee get involved in political, religious or trade union organizations?

Yes, so long as the role neither disturbs operations at the workplace nor prevents the completion of work by employees. 175

Can an employer assign an employee to work at a different site, perform different work or both?

Such transfer, or relocation clauses are regularly found in employment contracts. What is decisive here is if the clause is proportional and reasonable to the employee. 176

Can an employer post an employee at another affiliate or company within their group?

177 Yes, so long as the given employment contract also allows for other affiliates and companies within the group to be arranged as work-sites. According to the German Temporary Employment Act, an internal transfer does not require permission if the employee is not going to be hired and employed for the purpose of being permanently transferred.

May the employer release the employee from having to work?

178 No, since along with the obligation to perform the work to be carried out comes the right to provide these services. The employer has to provide work for the employee and not solely pay him/her wages. This right is derived from the right to protection of one's individual sphere of life. The employer may only release the employee from having to work if the interest of the release from work is greater than the employer's interest for the performance of the work to be carried out. For instance this is the case with valid dismissals for operational reasons and the discontinuation of employment opportunity due to restructuring. The right to release from work because of dismissal can be explicitly agreed upon in the employment contract.

What needs to be observed with respect to business trips?

179 Employees are obligated to go on business trips if the employment contract includes them. This obligation does not have to be expressly agreed upon. It can arise out of the job description or line of work. The employer can also mandate business trips as part of his/her authority to give instructions per the obligations set out in the employment contract.

Are employees entitled to a company car?

180 No, unless the employee is granted a company car by contract. However, from the perspective of the German Employment law principle of equal treatment, the employee can be entitled to a company car if his co-workers in the same position have one.

May the employee have a company car for private use?

181 No, this is not required. Different regulations apply if such consent is provided in an individual employment contract or collective bargaining agreement.

Does the employer have to approve or possibly pay for an employee to pursue further professional training?

No, as no such legal obligation exists. The employer's obligation to approve or pay for further professional training can be the result of stipulations in an employment contract or collective bargaining or works agreement. If such a stipulation is missing, a right can arise out of the principle of equal treatment if the employer has approved training for employees in the same position. 182

If the employer pays for the further professional training, can he/she oblige the employee to reimburse these costs upon resignation?

That depends whether the employee gained an added value from the professional training, how expensive it was and for how long it lasted. A reimbursement clause has to take into account the level and duration of the reimbursement payments. 183

Are employees entitled to company housing?

No, but usage of a company housing can be promised to the employee in an employment contract. The right of use is then a part of the compensation package. In this case the termination of an employment contract cannot be isolated from the lease agreement. 184

What are preclusion periods?

Preclusion periods (aka "expiration periods" – Verfallsfristen) can be found in employment contracts, collective bargaining agreements and works agreements. Agreed to or statutorily protected rights expire by way of preclusion periods if assertion of the rights does not take place within the agreed time period and in the agreed form. Preclusion periods serve in this respect to shorten the three-year statutory limitation period that arises in employment relationships. Preclusion periods are to be observed officially through the courts without one party having to rely on it. They therefore hold a stronger and more detrimental effect for the affected party than the statute of limitations. 185

What can employers do against the illicit communication of (company) secrets?

Employers usually protect themselves with employment contract clauses that obligate the employer to secrecy with respect to company and trade secrets. This obligation to secrecy begins with the signing of the employment contract and does not end after the end of the employment relationship. The employer can also conclude a special non-disclosure agreement (Geheimhaltungsvertrag). This is subject to criminal law protection. In cases of illicit communication of a (company) secret, employ- 186 ees can be subject to three years imprisonment. Furthermore, the employer can explicitly state the need for secrecy or protect the corresponding files with passwords.

Does an employer operating in Germany have to establish a company-run daycare center?

187 No, as no such legal obligation exists in this respect. Different regulations apply if such consent is provided in an individual employment contract or collective bargaining agreement.

Does the employer have to offer company sports activities or a gym?

188 No, as no such legal obligation exists on this issue. Different regulations apply if such amenities are to be provided for per an individual employment contract or collective bargaining agreement.

Does the employer have to offer perks or benefits like "Jobtickets" (for public transportation), reduced-cost lunches or health exams?

189 No, as no such legal obligation exists in this respect. Different regulations apply if consent is provided in an individual employment contract or collective bargaining agreement.

To what extent does the employer have duty to provide health care and benefits?

190 The general duty to provide health care and benefits that employers have obligates them to act accordingly, as "employer", meaning that they have to keep the employee's interest in mind, safeguarding the company's interest and that of other employees in a way that appears correct and fair in view of the principle of good faith. This is determined by the need for protection of each employee, which increases with a view to the length of service to the company or the position of trust. The duty to provide health care and benefits begins taking effect during the contract negotiation phase, with issues like the duty to explain the employee-employer relationship to be expected. Furthermore, there is a legal duty to explain how German social security works, and the employer has a responsibility for employee welfare that includes providing leave for job search, information about former employees, issuance of working papers as well as the preparation of references. The employer is also committed to the care of the employee's life and health. He/she has to avert avoidable disadvantages to the employee.

What duties of fidelity exist for the employee?

Out of employment, an employee has an obligation to work. There are also secondary obligations for the employee in order to safeguard the protection-worthy interests of the employer. There are individual restrictive covenants, but also obligations to carry out favorable actions. The employee may not share with a third party any trade or company secrets. Based on the employee obligation of secrecy and non-disclosure, the employee is to refrain from communicating information that could harm one's reputation or credit. The employee may not accept bribes ("handshake money"). Further, the employee may not compete with his/her employer in the employer's given area of business. Employees are also affected by their duties to disclose and report about matters such as a pending loss. In addition to this, the employee has a duty to obey the employer. 191

Can an employee refuse to perform work?

Without a special reason, basically not. A refusal to perform work can entitle the employer to terminate the employment contract and demand damages. That said the employee is entitled to refuse to do work if the employee finds him/herself in a situation where performing the given task may be actually possible but the employer cannot demand fulfillment of the task due to overriding aspects. An example of this would be if the employee finds himself in a moral conflict due to the work to be performed. 192

Are employees entitled to a part-time work?

Yes, but a requirement for this is that the employee has been working for the given employer for at least six months. The application for part-time work can only be made biennially. 193

When do claims arising out of an employment contract come under the statute of limitations and expire?

The statutes of limitations run from three months to as long as thirty years. After three months, all employer claims regarding the employee's anti-competition violations against the employer because of the employer's knowledge of the business lapse. After thirty years the statute of limitations for claims for return of property expires regarding ownership and other property rights. However, the general statute of limitations is three years. 194

Vacation/Urlaub

Definition, Legal Principles

195 Every employee in Germany has a legal right to paid vacation. This is regulated by the Federal Paid Leave Act (Bundesurlaubsgesetz). The minimum amount of vacation time German law allows is 24 days per annum based on a six-day work week. Other special vacation regulations arise out of agreements stipulated in individual contract or collective bargaining agreements. Due to these regulations, those working full-time in Germany have an average of 28–30 vacation days per year.

196 The severely handicapped have a right to take an additional paid work week off each year. Youth workers also have a right to more vacation time.

197 Basically, all employment relationships can grant extra paid leave. The granting of extra paid leave can be tied to the length of service or certain events, such as the employee's birthday.

How many vacation days does an employee working in Germany have per calendar year on average?

198 Usually, workers in Germany have 30 vacation days per calendar year. This correlates to a six-week vacation for a five-day work week.

How many vacation days per calendar year does German law require employees to have?

199 The German Federal Leave Act grants employees in Germany a legal right to at least 24 work days of vacation. The rule is based off of a six-day work week. There is a conversion of the legally provided vacation days on the basis of a five-day work week. In accordance with this, there is a right to 20 work days, in other words four weeks.

Example: 24 working days off for vacation: 6-day work week; 20 working days off for vacation: 5-day work week

Is the employee entitled to paid leave beyond his/her vacation entitlement?

200 Yes, but entitlement to such leave exists only if the employee is unable to work due to urgent personal reasons. The employee retains his/her right to compensation, for example, in case of family events (his/her own wedding, birth of a child, religious celebrations, like a child's first communion, or funerals of close relatives), obligations of honorary office or appointments with public authorities/court dates. In cases of death, the day of the funeral and the days of the death itself will be granted as extra paid leave. If an employee's child becomes ill, that mother or father will be

granted up to five days of extra paid leave. For weddings the employee has the option to choose the civil ceremony, church ceremony or both as a two-day block.[36]

Does the employer have to pay wages to employees who are on vacation?

The entitlement to vacation time represents the claim to a paid vacation. The amount of the vacation pay is calculated in terms of the average earned income the employee earned during the thirteen weeks prior to the vacation. 201

Does the employer have to pay the employee an extra vacation allowance (Urlaubsgeld)?

No, as no legal obligation to pay the employee an extra vacation allowance exists. However, it is often the case that collective bargaining and works agreements provides for this and the payment of vacation allowance is often observed. 202

When does an employee gain the right to vacation time?

A six-month employment relationship with the given employer within a calendar year is required for a right to the entire legally permitted vacation time. If the employment relationship has been shorter than six months, then there is a claim to a pro-rated vacation time according to sec. 5 of the Federal Paid Leave Act that is reduced by percentages in accordance with the length of the employment relationship. According to this law, the duty of the employer to grant leave should comport with the actual time of employment. Without special rules to the contrary, the employee would not be entitled to vacation time if section 5 of the Federal Paid Leave Act were not in force because article 4 of the same law does not grant the right to full vacation time prior to the employee's sixth month of work. For each month the employment relationship exits, the employee earns $^{1}/_{12}$ of a full-year's vacation allotment. 203

At what point in the year is the amount of vacation an employee is entitled to determined?

A vacation year is a calendar year. The full annual vacation entitlement occurs on January 1 of a calendar year. 204

36 In Germany, a civil ceremony before a registrar of deaths, marriages and births is required for the marriage to be legally recognized. A church or other religious ceremony is a separate event that the couple may or may not elect to do.

Does vacation need to be taken over consecutive days or can it be spread out?

205 Vacation time has to be taken over consecutive days unless there is a work-related emergency or the particular employee's situation leaves the employer with grounds to make other arrangements. If the given vacation taken exceeds twelve work days (for a five-day work week, ten work days) and that vacation time is to be spread over different time periods, the specified vacation period has to include at least twelve (or ten) work days.

When does the employee have to take vacation?

206 The vacation time due has to be taken during the course of the given calendar year and may only be taken during the next calendar year in cases of a work-related emergency or the particular employee's situation leaves the employer with reason to make other arrangements. If the vacation due is carried over to the next calendar year, it has to be taken in the first three months of that year.

When do vacation days expire?

207 Vacation days expire when they are not taken within a calendar year in which they were accrued or within the first three months of the following years into which they were carried over.

Do employees have to fill out a vacation request form?

208 There is no legally mandated formal requirement for vacation requests. A written request alone serves to provide proof and should therefore be used for vacation requests.

May an employee perform the duties of an honorary office or work elsewhere during a vacation period?

209 Employment during a vacation is forbidden. The employee may not perform a job that contradicts with the fact that he/she is supposed to be on vacation. Other rules apply only if the purpose of the vacation is not affected by the other activity during the vacation period. So, for example, an activity exercised on a regular basis can be performed during a vacation. An honorary office that does not stand in the way of the employee's relaxation (the purpose of vacation from a German perspective) does not violate the ban on working during a vacation.

What happens if the employee becomes ill during his/her vacation?

If the employee becomes ill during a vacation period, the days that the employee is unable to work due to illness will not be counted as vacation days. A doctor's note that attests that illness would have prevented the employee from working is required. It is immaterial whether the employee can relax despite the illness. The number of days on which the illness prevents the employee from working has to be granted again as vacation to that employee. 210

What happens if, due to a long-term illness, the employee can neither take the vacation due within the given current calendar year nor is able to use the time in the first three months of the following year?

In cases like this, the claim to the given vacation time does not expire on March 31st of the following year; it expires instead 15 months after the end of the vacation year in question. 211

Once the employee who suffered a long-term illness can work again, what rule(s) apply with respect to his/her vacation time?

Carried over vacation time of an employee who had been ill for a long time is subject to the regular guidelines, which means that the given vacation time has to be taken during that current calendar year and can only be carried over if used by March 31st of the following calendar year. 212

Can an employee waive his/her right to vacation time?

No, waiver of minimum vacation time is not possible. Vacation serving to as a means of relaxation and recovery cannot be individually or collectively contractually precluded. Such an agreement is invalid. 213

Can the employer shorten someone's vacation time in cases of, for example, illness or pregnancy?

No, the right to vacation days is dependent from the existence of the employment relationship alone. The length of time services have been carried out is not important. 214

Can the employer mandate a closure for annual vacation?

Yes, but the employer has to observe employees' desired dates for taking their own vacation. The employer can base this closure on his/her wishes and deviate from those of the employees for urgent company concerns. 215

What happens if the employment relationship ends and the employee was unable to take the allowed vacation time beforehand?

216 In these cases the entitlement to vacation time is converted into one for compensation. This entitlement to compensation is a substitute for the vacation time not realized and is calculated like vacation pay would be: the average earned income the employee earned during the thirteen weeks prior to the vacation, or, in this case, before the conclusion of the employment relationship.

What applies to vacation time that had been carried over from the previous year due to a lengthy illness if the employment relationship ends?

217 Even carried-over vacation time is converted into an entitlement to compensation.

What happens to the vacation entitlement if the employment relationship ends because of the death of the employee?

218 If the employment relationship ends with the employee's death, the vacation entitlement expires at that time. It is not converted into an entitlement to compensation for the benefit of the heirs.

What special rules apply for teenaged employees?

219 German laws considers teens those working who are 15 but are not yet 18. For this the German Youth Employment Protection Act applies. According to that law, the annual legal entitlement to vacation time is:

- at least 30 workdays if the teen is not yet 16 by the beginning of the given calendar year;
- at least 27 work days if the teen is not 17 by the beginning of the given calendar year;
- at least 25 work days if the teen is not yet 18 by the beginning of the given calendar year.

220 Teens who work in the mining industry receive additional vacation time of three work days.

221 Apart from that the fundamental regulations set out in the German Federal Leave Act apply as appropriate.

What special rules apply for students of vocational schools?

For adult students of vocational schools the Federal Leave Act regulations apply.

Teen students of vocational schools should be given vacation time during the time of their school break. So long as there is a school break at the given vocational school, each day attended there during the usual vocational school break earns the teen an additional day of vacation. 222

Do severely handicapped persons have a right to additional vacation?

Yes, severely handicapped persons have a right to additional vacation, five extra days per calendar year. This does not apply to those who are, for example considered partially handicapped. 223

The entitlement to additional vacation time increases and decreases accordingly if the regular working times of the severely handicapped person are spread over a work week that is more than or less than a five-day calendar work week. If the severely handicapped status is not present for the entire calendar year, the severely handicapped person is entitled to a twelfth of the extra vacation time for each whole calendar month he/she is in the employment relationship with severely handicapped status, and fractional amounts of vacation days that amount to at least one-half work day are to be rounded up to a full day. 224

If the status of being a severely handicapped person is established retroactively, German Employment law regulations establishing grounds for the employment relationship find application for carrying the extra vacation time over into the next calendar year. 225

Working Hours/Arbeitszeit

Definition, Legal Principles

Working Hours in Germany are regulated by the German Working Hours Act (Arbeitszeitrecht), which addresses different regulatory subject matters, including the establishment of boundaries within which those setting contractual working hours rules can operate. What is specifically set is the maximum working hours, length of breaks and rest periods and regulations regarding the timeframes for work, including work on Sundays and holidays. 226

The purpose of law protecting working times and above all the German Working Hours Act itself is to guaranty the health and safety for employees in the organization with reasonable working times and to improve the general conditions for flexible working times. The maximum number of hours allowed to be worked is regulated by the Working Hours Act and some other protective acts governed by public law. 227

The weekly amount of hours to be worked is found in collective bargaining agreements and individual employment agreements. These agreements also determine what working times will be considered compensated and whether the em- 228 ployee has to work overtime. Daily working times and hours to be worked are determined by the employer per his/her supervisory authority over employees.

229 But, employers have to observe the participatory rights held by the works council in this context. The works council has co-determination rights regarding the time for the beginning and end of the working day, as well as breaks and overtime or temporary reduction of working hours.

What is generally included in the working hour regulations?

230 To differentiate, there are three areas:
- the German Working Hours Act,
- the contractual working hour regulations, and
- the working hour regulations related to co-determination rights.

231 The rules regarding German working-hours regulations, especially the Working Hours Act (Arbeitszeitgesetz), standardize binding general legal requirements for employee working hours. The contractual working hour regulations determine during which time periods the employee has to produce or perform his/her work, as well as what claim he/she has to compensation pursuant to agreements. The working hour regulations related to co-determination rights regulate the scope of employee rights of participation that the works council has according to the German Works Constitution Act (Betriebsverfassungsgesetz).

How long may an employee in Germany work and how are weekly working hours arranged in Germany?

232 The legally permitted maximum working hours for an employee is eight hours per workday. Workdays include all days of the week except for Sunday and legal holidays, which may vary from state to state in Germany. The Working Hours Act is based on a six-day-week and weekly working hours totaling 48 hours. The daily working hours can be extended to ten hours if it is within six calendar months or within 24 weeks, and an average of eight hours per day will not be exceeded.

What is the difference between overtime and excess hours worked?

233 German Federal Labor Court speaks of "overtime compensated with time in lieu" (i.e. flextime) or "paid overtime" if the agreed upon working hours for the particular employment relationship are exceeded, which would be those set by collective or individual agreement.

234 "Excess hours worked" are understood as those extra hours worked that exceed the legally permissible maximum working hours.

Does an employee have to work overtime hours?

There is no legal obligation. Overtime is only to be worked in extraordinary circumstances i.e. emergencies. However, the employee and employer can adjust the employment contract so that the employee has to work overtime. If this is the case, the employer is authorized to instruct the employee at any time to work overtime without extra notification. 235

What happens if the employee does not work the permissibly mandated overtime hours?

If the employee refuses to perform permissibly mandated overtime hours, terminating the employment relationship is justifiable. That said, the employee has to have been warned beforehand. 236

Does the employer have to compensate for overtime worked by a salaried employee?

There is no legal rule to pay extra compensation for automatic overtime or each instance of presence for work that is above the agreed-upon or typical working hours for a said company. If there is no rule about compensation in the employment contract, the issue of whether or not there is an obligation to compensate for overtime exists needs to be determined. It has to involve mandated or authorized overtime. Case law requires a particularly higher amount of work from highly paid employees, even if the typical working hours of a given company is exceeded by working those extra hours. 237

Can overtime be compensated by a lump-sum payment?

There is a 20% rule with average wages. That means that up to eight overtime hours a week based on a 40-hour working week would count as compensated with such a payment. 238

Does the employer have to compensate for overtime worked by an hourly-wage employee?

With hourly wages, compensation for overtime with the basic rate of pay goes without question. The agreement of a monthly wage being simultaneously set for when the amount of the working time is, justifies the conclusion that the agreement applies to monthly compensation for the work performed by the employee within the agreed-upon time period. Further, overtime has to be paid based on the portion of the monthly salary that corresponds to one hour of work. 239

May an employee work at night?

240 Yes, the permissibility of working night hours is based on the German Working Hours Act. The working times of employees working at night is further determined according to the verified ergonomic studies' findings about work that determined to be adequately designed for humans. For employees working at night the principle of eight-hour workdays with the possibility of extending to ten hours applies, but with a shorter comp time period from a calendar month or of four weeks. Employees working at night are entitled to have themselves medically examined before beginning working these hours and in regular intervals after that point.

What models for working times are there?

241 There are
- time-credit accounts,
- flextime systems, and
- working time based on an honors system.

How do time-credit accounts (Arbeitszeitkonten) in Germany work?

242 With the general term time-credit account, a wide range of different models for increased flexibility of working times are understood. There are two basic types that are common:
- annual-hours contracts;
- set-aside accounts.

What is an annual-hours contract?

243 On the basis of annual-hours contracts, the employment contract can determine a set volume of work to be spread over an annual planning period instead of a weekly or monthly one. That way it is possible to plan flexibly foreseeably long-term, but intermittent working needs within a one-year period.

How does a set-aside account work in Germany?

244 Set-aside accounts open the opportunity to the employee to save hours worked above regular work hours for a transition period outside of his/her regular work life, despite the continuation of the employment relationship. The account may be used for things such as extended vacation time, continuing education or training or early partial or full retirement, and the employee still receives his/her full salary.

How does flextime work in Germany?

Only during a particular, set core working time does an attendance requirement exist for the employee. Besides this, the employee can freely use his/her time outside of the time period during which the flextime is to be worked. 245

What is meant by working hours based on an honors system?

The employer foregoes recording time worked and other forms of direct checks on working time. Time management and attendance at the workplace are stipulated at the discretion of the employee. Individual targets are defined work results and objectives. 246

What rest periods in work does the employee have to take?

Rest periods for the employee are set by statute. For working periods of six to nine hours, there must be a 30-minute rest period; for working periods above nine hours there must be a 45-minute break. A break must be at least 15 minutes, otherwise it counts as working time. The Working Hours Act does not define the term break. According to German Federal Labor Court, this deals with a pre-planned break in work in which the employee can freely decide where and how he or she will spend this time. The employee has to be exempted from having to perform work of any kind during such breaks. 247

May work take place on Sundays and government holidays?

Generally, not. The making employees work on Sundays and government holidays is forbidden for all areas of employment. This is a result of the constitutional requirement of Sunday being a day of rest (Sonntagsruhe) and that the statutory holiday rest periods be observed. The ban on employees working on Sundays and government holidays is not dispositive. Individual or collective agreements, which contravene this work ban are null and void. However, the German Working Hours Act includes a comprehensive catalog of areas in which employees may work on Sundays or government holidays so long as the work cannot be performed on a traditional workday. 248

Which statutory rest times does the employee have to take?

For the employee an uninterrupted rest period of at least eleven hours after the end of daily working hours is to be observed. Working Hours Act does not provide a legal definition of rest period. A rest period means, however, that the period of time between the end of daily working hours and the start of the next period of daily working hours. 249

Is travel to work (travel time) work time?

250 No, it is not. The time that the employee spends traveling to and from work is in the private sphere and therefore associated with a rest period. Travel time for travel from the place of business to and from an off-site place of business is counted as regular working hours. The same can apply for both ways of travel for business trips.

What is meant by Germans with "readiness to work" (Arbeitsbereitschaft)?

251 "Readiness to work" is defined by the German Federal Labor Court as a sort of work that does not entirely engage the employee, and thus does not require his/her full attention. Some examples include taxi or limo drivers who are waiting to take a client somewhere or a fire fighter who is awaiting a call to duty. Here, the employer has sent the employee to work, and the employee, though awake, can relax, for being ready to work represents a minimal performance of work compared to full performance of work.

252 Readiness to work has to be distinguished from rest period. In the latter, the employee is not obligated to keep him/herself in a constant state of wakeful attentiveness to commence work.

What is meant by on stand-by work?

253 This is the time period during which the employee has to stay in a particular place within or outside of the place of business for business reasons. In this manner the employee can start working as needed, be that immediately or promptly. To be on stand-by is not the full performance of work, but instead a limitation on where the employee can be (how far from the place of work, for example); and this comes with the obligation to commence work without delay when needed. Stand-by work counts as working hours.

How counts as being on-call in Germany?

254 Being on-call obligates the employee to commence work when phoned. In comparison to stand-by work, the employee can remain at a place of his/her choice that the employer is aware of. The employee has to ensure that he/she may be reached at any time. Being on-call counts towards the employee's working hours.

What counts as shift work?

255 Shift work is not statutorily regulated. According to the Federal Labor Court, however, shift work exists if the work tasks is completed as an employee's daily work over an extended period and performed by several employees in a set chronological order. For shift work the general provisions of working hours applies. Shift work can

be introduced into all sectors of business. The German Working Hours Act contains an opening clause for collective agreements. Beyond that the Working Hours Act does not have special regulations. So long as the employee works both day and night shifts, the regulations for working at night apply.

Does the employer have an obligation to report?

Yes, the employer is obligated to make a copy of the Federal Working Hours Act 256
visible for inspection in suitable workplace areas or to give employees copies.

Does the employer have an obligation to keep records?

Yes, the employer has to keep records about hours worked that surpass those on 257
normal work days (i.e. overtime). Not covered here are working hours of up to eight hours on workdays (Monday to Saturday).

Part 3
Social Security

I. Introduction to the German social security system

When companies assign their employees to work abroad, the social security law 1
situation should be explained to all parties involved before the work in the foreign country commences. Who should explain it? It is in fact important to remember that, as a rule, the obligation to verify and process social security lies with the employer in Germany, so the responsibility typically lies with the HR department. The issues are diverse, and include avoiding legal sanctions due to unpaid social security contributions or maintaining insurance coverage of the employee and his or her family members. To begin, one needs to keep the following general points in mind with respect to social security:

- INBOUND – Foreign employers whose employees are sent on foreign assignment to work in Germany in some cases have to register and contribute to German social security during the expat's foreign assignment.
- OUTBOUND – German employers who send their employees on foreign assignment have the opportunity to ensure that their employees remain in the German social security system during the employee's time abroad.

II. EU/EEA-States and Switzerland

1 **Although there are advantages to being assigned to or from most European countries to another due to open border policies, there are still some clear guidelines within Europe that employers and employees need to bear in mind when considering where to make social security contributions, for example. Dating back to 1958, the European Council has been working out rules on coming to terms with social security matters and the increasingly free movement of workers. With about 10% of EU citizens working across various EU borders, it is critical that employers and employees be familiar with certain regulations, such as (EC) No. 883/2004, so has to avoid legal difficulties. This section will address this EU-wide regulation many of the concerns dealing with social security, in order to become aware of where there may be pitfalls assignees and their respective companies should attempt avoiding.**

For foreign assignments within the EU, EEA, or Switzerland, with what law is the application of social security regulations aligned?

2 The application of social security regulations is in accordance with Regulation (EC) No. 883/2004, which coordinates the social security systems within the EU.

Which countries are included within the scope of Regulation (EC) No. 883/2004?

3 Austria, Belgium, Bulgaria, Croatia, Cyprus, Czech Republic, Denmark, Estonia, Finland, France, Germany, Greece, Hungary, Iceland, Ireland, Italy, Latvia, Liechtenstein, Lithuania, Luxembourg, Malta, Netherlands, Norway, Poland, Portugal, Romania, Slovakia, Slovenia, Spain, Sweden, Switzerland, United Kingdom.

Which people are included within the scope of Regulation (EC) No. 883/2004?

4 Generally speaking, these are:
- EU citizens;
- people who are not citizens of an EU country but who possess legally recognized residency in an EU member state, referred to as third-country nationals (Drittstaatsangehörige).

5 Note that special rules exist for third-country nationals with relation to Norway, Denmark, Great Britain, Iceland, Liechtenstein and Switzerland.

What benefits are included within the scope of Regulation (EC) No. 883/2004?

Regulation (EC) No. 883/2004 affords the following benefits: 6

- services when ill, including continued remuneration;
- maternity benefits and equal parental benefits for fathers (e.g. parental leave);
- disability benefits;
- old-age benefits;
- survivor benefits;
- work-related injuries and illnesses;
- death/funeral benefit;
- unemployment benefits;
- early-retirement benefits;
- family benefit (parental-leave allowance, child allowance).

1. Inbound

When is an employee on foreign assignment in Germany subject to German social security regulations?

According to the "principle of territoriality" (jus soli), an employee is subject to the 7
social security regulations of the country in which he or she is physically working, which is Germany in this case. Special rules apply to a few professions (e.g. civil servant, Multi-State Workers).

Are there exceptions to the principle of territoriality?

Yes. If the conditions for the assignment set forth in Regulation (EC) No. 883/2004 8
have been fulfilled, the employee on assignment in Germany is not subject to German social security regulations. This means that he or she if not obligated to participate in or contribute to German social security insurance.

What are the conditions determining that an employee is on foreign assignment set forth in Regulation (EU) 883/2004?

Regulation (EC) No. 883/2004 stipulates that someone is considered to be on foreign 9
assignment, particularly in cases where a person is:

- in an EU member state on behalf of an employer with business operations/ working there;
- performing work;
- was sent to another member state by that employer.

In order to complete a job on that employer's behalf there. Further, the estimated 10
duration of the work to be performed may not exceed 24 months, and the person on

that particular assignment is not replacing another person on assignment to perform the same work for the same company.

If the conditions set forth in Regulation (EC) No. 883/2004 are met, does an application to be exempt from the German social security regulations have to be submitted?

11 Yes, an application needs to be submitted in the assignee's home country at the office responsible for such matters. As a rule, that office is the social security insurance administrator. If the requirements for a legally recognized foreign assignment exist, a certificate for the legal regulations to be applied – the "A1 certificate" – has to be verified. The A1 certificate serves as proof that the foreign country's (that is, the assignee's home country's) social security rules apply to the assignee during the time he or she is assigned to work in Germany. Beyond that, the assigned employee is freed from applying German social security insurance rules (e.g. to the statutory pension, health, long-term care, unemployment and accident insurance). That means, for the employee assigned to work in Germany, there is no obligation to contribute to German social security insurance, and the foreign employer does not have to collect German social security contributions in Germany.

What consequences arise if the requirements for a legally recognized foreign assignment per Regulation (EC) No. 883/2004 are not met? Do German social security contributions still need to be collected for the expat?

12 There is the possibility of being freed from having to apply German social security regulations as part of an Agreement of Exemption (Ausnahmevereinbarung). Whether the conditions for an Agreement of Exemption exist or not is checked by the office responsible for such matters in the employee's home country, not in Germany.

What are the consequences if the A1 certificate has not been presented?

13 If form A1 has not been presented, German social security rules apply for the time expat is working in Germany. This means that the foreign employer in this case would have contribution and registration obligations, and would thus need to submit contributions to German social security authorities. A foreign employer in this situation is required to register with the German Federal Employment Agency (Bundesagentur für Arbeit) and the German Institution for Statutory Accident Insurance and Prevention (Berufsgenossenschaft) for social security law purposes in order for the appropriate German social security contributions (employer and employee part) to be collected. If there is a local German employment contract with a German company, the contribution and registration obligation has to be adhered to by the German company. German authorities determine on a case-by-case basis

whether and which type of social security benefits present an obligation to insure (and therefore applies to a given employee assigned to work in Germany).

2. Outbound

Does an employee assigned from Germany to another country continue to be subject to German social security regulations?

According to the principle of territoriality, such an employee is subject to the social security regulations of the country where he or she is physically located to work, outside of Germany in this case. This means that, if an employee does not carry out his or her work within Germany's borders, he or she is no longer subject to German social security regulations. It should be noted, however, that there are some professions that fall under different rules (e.g. civil servants, multi-state workers). 14

Are there exceptions to the principle of territoriality?

Yes, if the requirements for foreign assignments set forth in Regulation (EC) No. 883/2004 have been satisfied, then the employee posted to work on foreign assignment is still subject to German social security regulations. 15

What are some of the more specific requirements for a foreign assignment Regulation (EC) No. 883/2004 sets forth?

According to Regulation (EC) No. 883/2004, a foreign assignment exists if its employee regularly employed by that company: 16

- is regularly carrying work in another EU-member state;
- was assigned by his or her employer to carry out that work;
- is working in that other EU-member state on behalf of the employer who sent the employee;
- has been assigned to work in the EU-member state for under 24 months;
- is not replacing someone else on foreign assignment who had been performing the same work.

The employer is considered operating regularly in Germany if it carries out at least 25% of its business in Germany. This 25% is determined by a measuring the portion of revenue and employees working in Germany. 17

Beyond that, Regulation (EC) No. 883/2004 stipulates that an employee has to be subject German social security regulations immediately prior to commencing his or her foreign assignment. If a local (foreign) employment contract and a suspended German employment contract exist, it is assumed that the job in the other EU-member state is not being carried out on behalf of a Germany employer. 18

If the conditions for a foreign assignment per Regulation (EC) No. 883/2004 exist, does an application to be subject to the German social security regulations still need to be submitted?

19 Yes, an application needs to be submitted to the appropriate office in Germany. Then, the A1 certificate has to be issued by the statutory health insurance office in Germany. As mentioned earlier, the A1 certificate serves as proof that German social security regulations are applied during the time work is carried out in Germany. Further, the employee on foreign assignment is exempted from any foreign social security regulations. That means that the German employer still needs to collect the appropriate German social security contributions from its employee on foreign assignment.

What questions arise if the conditions for a foreign assignment per Regulation (EC) No. 883/2004 are not present?

20 There is still a possibility that German social security regulations can take effect per an agreement of exemption. Whether the conditions for an Agreement of Exemption exist or not is checked by the German office responsible for such matters.

What questions arise if the A1 certificate has not been presented?

21 If the A1 certificate has not been presented, German social security regulations do not apply, and the foreign European country's do. This means that the German employer has to observe the contribution and registration rules abroad. In this case, the German employer has to register with the foreign social security administration and collect the appropriate contributions. Which social security category or categories apply – or whether there is an obligation in the first place – has to be determined by the foreign country's laws on the subject.

III. Countries with which German has a social security treaty

In 1883, Germany became the first nation to enact legislation on a type, or branch, of social security insurance. Many nations would follow suit. For example, between 1919 and 1927, not only Germany codified unemployment rules. So, too, did Australia, Austria, Bulgaria, Italy, Luxembourg, Poland, the Irish Free State, as well as several Swiss cantons.[37] Today, there are dozens more, and Germany has social security agreements with these so-called *Abkommenstaaten*, or contracting (or treaty) states. These may have social security insurance systems that are similar to Germany's but nevertheless necessitate recognition of equivalencies, an especially critical point for those working on foreign assignment as well as those expatriating and inpatriating employees. 1

This section addresses what social security rules apply to the *Abkommenstaaten*. Foreign assignees – as well as the companies they represent – sent to work in Germany from these nations are held to the terms of their corresponding agreement on social security matters. The same applies to those assigned sent to work in the contracting states who were working with a German contract. 2

To serve this end, this section covers at first some basic concepts under German law and then moves on to look at inbounding and outbounding employees. 3

What is an "Abkommensstaat" under German law?

An "Abkommensstaat" in this context is a country with which Germany shares a contractual relationship in the area of social security. Hereinafter, they will be referred to as contracting countries. 4

With which countries does Germany have a social security treaty?

Beyond EU agreements, German is the signatory to social security treaties with Australia, Bosnia-Herzegovina, Brazil, Chile, China, India, Israel, Japan, Canada, Korea, Kosovo, Morocco, Macedonia, Montenegro, Quebec, Serbia, Turkey, Tunisia, Uruguay, and the USA. 5

---

37 Abe Bortz, "Social Security: A Brief History of Social Insurance," http://socialwelfare.library.vcu.edu/social-security/social-security-a-brief-history-of-social-insurance/.

Which individuals does this type of agreement cover?

6 Principally, such an agreement covers all people who are working in a treaty-partner nation without consideration to citizenship. Special rules have been set forth in the treaties between Tunisia, Morocco, and Turkey.

What type of social security benefits does such an agreement cover?

7 As a rule, social security treaties always cover the area of retirement insurance. Whether other types of social security benefits are covered depends on the stipulations set forth in the particular treaty.

1. Inbound

Are those employees posted on foreign assignment in Germany subject to German social security rules?

8 The application of German social security rules accords the principle of territoriality as regulated by the particular treaty in question. This principally means that an employee on foreign assignment is subject to the legal regulation of the partner nation in whose territory the employee is carrying out his or her work (in this case, Germany). Be aware, however, that such a treaty can contain special rules for certain business sectors. It would be wise to seek counsel on those specifics as they arise (e.g. for employees of a flight crew).

What are the requirements for a foreign assignment set forth in a social security treaty?

9 For our purposes here, as a rule, such a treaty regulates the requirements for determining what a foreign assignment is. Generally, an employee on foreign assignment to work in Germany has to have been sent to work within the borders of another contracting (treaty) country in order to carry out the fixed-term work he or she planned to perform prior to arrival in that contracting country. This work must be in line with his or her employment relationship with the employer, the one sending the employee on foreign assignment.

10 Additionally, employees are required to have been subject to German social security immediately prior to going on foreign assignment. If both a local employment contract abroad and a dormant employment contract in the employee's home country (here Germany) exist, it is assumed that the employee is not on foreign assignment in the other contracting nation in the context of his or her German employment relationship. Instead, he or she is considered as being employed in the other contracting country.

Are there exceptions to the principle of territoriality when it comes to social security treaties between nations?

Yes, if the requirements for a foreign assignment have been fulfilled in accordance with treaty in question, the employee on foreign assignment in Germany is not subject to German social security regulations. This means that there is no social security obligation in Germany for the types of social security benefits noted in the treaty. Special rules apply to the agreements between Israel and Turkey. 11

What requirements need to be met for a foreign assignment to be recognized in a social security treaty?

Every contracting nation defines the particular treaty's requirements necessary for a foreign assignment to be recognized. Generally, every employee who is working in a contracting country (here, outside of Germany) in the course of working for his or her employer in the other contracting country (here, Germany) is considered to be on foreign assignment. That job has to have rules set on what constitutes a foreign assignment prior to the employee arriving in other contracting country (here, Germany). 12

If the requirements set forth in the treaty have been met, does an application to be exempt from the types of German social security covered by the treaty have to be submitted?

Yes, an application needs to be submitted in the assignee's home country at the office responsible for these matters. As a rule, that office is the social security insurance administrator. A Certificate of Coverage will prove if the requirements for a foreign assignment have been met. The Certificate of Coverage serves as evidence that the types of social security benefits covered by the treaty are to be applied for the term of the posted employee's foreign assignment. 13

Further, there is an exemption from the application of German social security regulations for those types of social security benefits covered by the treaty. This means that employees assigned to work in Germany have no social security obligation in Germany and their respective employers are not obligated to contribute to the German social security system. 14

What questions arise if the requirements set forth in a treaty for foreign assignment are not met?

Obtaining an exemption from German social security rules is possible. This would apply to those types of social security benefits covered by a treaty with an Agreement of Exception. Whether the requirements for an Agreement of Exemption exist is determined by the office in the home country of the person assigned to work in Germany that is responsible for such matters. 15

What questions arise if there is no Certificate of Coverage?

16 If no Certificate of Coverage exists, German social security regulations need to be followed for the duration of the foreign assignment. This means that the foreign employer is obligated to report, collect, and pay in the appropriate social security contributions in Germany. Foreign employers in this case are required to register with the German Federal Employment Agency (Bundesagentur für Arbeit) and the German Institution for Statutory Accident Insurance and Prevention (Berufsgenossenschaft) for social security purposes, as well as withhold from their employees working in Germany the requisite amount of German social security contributions. If a local works agreement with a German company is in force, that company has the obligation report and make social security contributions in Germany. In which or if certain types of social security benefits for an employee on foreign assignment in Germany fall under German social security regulations is checked on a case-by-case basis.

What laws apply when determining the application of German rules on types of social security benefits that are not covered in a treaty?

17 The rules on whether and where German social security laws apply are in German Social Security Code, Book IV, sections 3, 4, and 5. For more, see questions to part 3 under "3.1. Inbound."

2. Outbound

Is an employee on assignment to work outside of Germany still subject to German social security regulations?

18 The application of German social security regulations is to be made in accordance with the principle of territoriality. Generally, an employee is subject to the laws of the country in whose territory he or she is carrying out work, which, in this case, is a country other than Germany. This in turn means that employees working outside of Germany are not usually subject to German social security regulations. A social security treaty can contain special rules for certain professions (e.g. employees of a flight crew).

Are there exceptions to the principle of territoriality?

19 Yes. If requirements for a foreign assignment set forth in the treaty have been met, the employee on assignment outbound from Germany is still subject to German social security laws. Special rules, however, do exist in the treaties Germany has with Israel and Turkey.

If there are requirements for a foreign assignment set forth in the treaty, does an application need to be filed? And, if so, with whom does it need to be filed?

Yes, an application must be filed with the office responsible for such matters in Germany, which typically is a statutory (state) health insurance fund (gesetzliche Krankenkasse). The German statutory (state) health insurance fund subsequently has to provide a Certificate of Coverage. The Certificate of Coverage serves as proof that German regulations regarding those types of social security benefits stipulated in the treaty that apply for the term of the foreign assignment. 20

Consequently, there is an exemption to using foreign regulations for those types of social security benefits covered by the treaty. This means that the German employer of the employee on assignment to work outside of Germany is still responsible for deducting the appropriate social security contributions from that employee's wages during the foreign assignment. 21

What are the consequences if the requirements for a foreign assignment set forth in the treaty have not been met?

There is still a possibility with an Agreement of Exception made within the framework of the treaty to prompt the application of German social security regulations. Such situations would only be assessed on a case-by-case basis. 22

What are the consequences for not having a Certificate of Coverage?

In cases where there is no Certificate of Coverage, non-German social security regulations would apply. This means that the German employer would need to be aware of any social security registration, wage deduction, and contribution rules in that foreign country. In such case, the German company has to register in the foreign country for social security purposes and collect the social security contributions appropriate for that employee in that country. Also, be aware that the host country's laws determine whether and for which types of social security benefits there is an obligation to insure one's self in the host country. 23

What specific laws stipulate the continued use of German social security regulations for types of social security benefits not covered in the treaty?

The continued application of German social security is determined by German laws codified in German Social Security Code, Book IV, sections 3, 4, and 5. For more, see questions to part 3 under "3.2. Outbound." 24

IV. Rest of the world

1 **With Germany having the world's fourth largest GDP, it only follows that it also has numerous bi- and multi-lateral social security agreements, many of which having been generally touched upon in this section. These agreements are in place to clarify and ease the process of determining how much, what type, or if any social security needs to me collected. This, of course, becomes a more challenging process if no agreement is in place. This section addresses how to address social security issues with such nations.**

2 **To serve this end, this section looks at first some basic concepts under German law and then moves on to look out inbounding and outbounding employees to non-contract.**

Which countries are considered non-contracting foreign states (Vertragsloses Ausland) for Germany?

3 Non-contracting foreign states refer to those countries that have no contractual (treaty) relationship regarding social security between Germany and that foreign country. That includes all countries outside of the EU/EEC and Switzerland, with the exception of those countries covered under question 18 of this chapter.

According to what rules or laws are German social security regulations applied for a foreign assignment in cases between outbounds coming from Germany to a noncontracting foreign state?

4 Domestic German law determines whether German social security regulations apply. More specifically, the relevant regulations are stipulated in the German Social Security Code, Book IV, secs. 3, 4 und 5.

1. Inbounds

Is an employee on foreign assignment in Germany subject to German social security regulations if he or she is from a non-contractual foreign state?

5 The application of German social security regulations is determined by the principle of territoriality, especially in such cases. Generally, the employee is subject to German social security regulations if he or she is carrying out work on German soil.

Are there exceptions to the principle of territoriality for those inbound from non-contractual foreign states?

Yes, if the conditions for inbound expat status per the German Social Security Code have been met, the employee on foreign assignment in Germany is not subject to German social security regulations. 6

What are the requirements for inbound status set forth in sec. 5, book IV of the German Social Security Code?

Under German social security law, an employee has inbound status exists in cases where there is a pre-exiting employment relationship outside of Germany and the limited duration of the work assignment in Germany is determined in advance. 7

When does German law recognize that there a foreign assignment in terms of inbound status?

There is a foreign assignment in terms of inbound status under German law if the employee goes from a foreign country and arrives in Germany on the instructions of his or her employer in order to carry out work for a pre-determined duration. 8

Under what circumstances is there a presumed to be a pre-existing employment relationship abroad?

A pre-existing employment relationship abroad exists when the foreign (non-German) employment contract remains in force during the tenure of the employees work in Germany. No employment relationship abroad is not assumed to exist if: 9

- the employer's payroll burden is carried by the hosting company during the term of the foreign assignment;
- the employee on foreign assignment in Germany has an employment contract with the German company.

When is a foreign assignment seen as having been time-limited in advance?

German law recognizes a time-limited foreign assignment as inpatriation if the end of the foreign assignment is prospectively foreseeable. More extensive time frames can be put into place due to the nature of the work to be performed (e.g. an audit, initial integration of billing software or platform) or by contract. 10

If the required conditions for an inbound status under German law have been satisfied, does an application to be exempt from the German social security scheme need to be made?

11 As a rule, there is no obligation – either by the employee or employer – to file an application to be exempt from the German social security scheme. The employer has to decide whether the employee assigned to work in Germany is subject to German social security regulations. In case there are doubts, the employer has the option to file an application for registering the employee's insurance assessment – per German social security guidelines – with the collecting agency (of a statutory health insurance) at the time the foreign employee is posted on assignment in Germany. For the following reasons, we recommend an application for establishing the existence of an inpatriation (inbound status) with the collecting agency be placed:

- Verification from the collecting agency provides both the foreign company and the German company with legal certainty vis-a-vis the location at which the employee on foreign assignment is placed.
- The foreign employer and host company have proof that there is no obligation to make social security contributions in Germany.
- This verification serves as documentation for company audits pursuant to German social security law, which are carried out on a regular basis.

The confirmation of an inpatriation applies for all types of social security benefits.

What are the consequences if the German legal requirements for an inpatriation have not been satisfied?

12 If the requirements for an inpatriation have not been satisfied, under German law, the foreign employer is obliged to keep in mind its registration and contribution obligations. This means that the foreign employer is required to register for social security in Germany (with either the German Federal Employment Agency or German Institution for Statutory Accident Insurance and Prevention) and pay the appropriate social security contributions to German authorities. If there is a local contract with a German company, the social security contribution and registration obligations of German companies apply to that company for that worker. Whether and for which types of German social security apply to an employee on foreign assignment in Germany is determined on a case-by-case basis.

2. Outbounds

Are employees outbound from Germany on foreign assignment still subject to German social security regulations while working abroad?

The application of German social security regulations is determined by the principle of territoriality. Generally, the employees on foreign assignment are subject to German social security laws if he or she carries out work on German soil. This means that if an employee does not carry out his or her work on German soil, no obligation to abide by German social security regulations exists. How the employee is covered by his or her social security system at home does not play a role here. 13

Are there exceptions to the principle of territoriality?

Yes, if the requirements for expatriation set forth in the German Social Security Code have been fulfilled, the employee n foreign assignment in Germany continues to be subject to German social security regulations. 14

What are the requirements for an expatriation (outbound status) according to the German Social Security Code?

Book IV of the German Social Security Code recognizes an expatriation if the foreign assignment in question is within the framework of an existing German employment relationship and the duration of the job abroad has a fixed term made in advance. 15

Under German law, when is does a foreign assignment exist in the sense of an expatriation?

An assignment in the sense of an expatriation under German law exists if the employee is working abroad at the behest of his employer in Germany in order to carry out a work assignment with a fixed-term duration that was set in advance. 16

Under which conditions is there presumed to be an existing German employment relationship?

German law recognizes there being an existing German employment relationship if the German employment contract is continues during the work assignment abroad. This means that the: 17

- German employment contract has not been either suspended or terminated, and
- the employee does not have an employment contract abroad.

18 German law does not recognize the existence of an employment relationship in Germany if the employee's salary costs are not borne by the German company during the foreign assignment, so that the salary costs are no longer be applied to German taxes as business costs by the German company.

When is a foreign assignment considered to be temporary under German law?

19 A fixed-term for a foreign assignment in the sense of an expatriation under German law exists if a foreseeable end can be prospectively seen. The pre-determined duration of the foreign assignment can be determined by the special nature of the work to be performed.

If the requirements for an expatriation under German law have been met, does an application to remain subject to the German social security scheme need to be made?

20 As a rule, neither the employee nor the employer is obligated to submit an application to remain subject to the German social security scheme. The employer can decide whether the employee on foreign assignment will continue to be subject to German social security regulations. In case of doubt, the employer has the option to file an application for requesting the employee social security assessment at the time of the foreign assignment to the office responsible for collecting social security contributions of the employee (a statutory health insurer). It is recommendable to request from authorities responsible for collecting social security contributions the confirmation of a legally recognized expatriation for the following reasons:

- The German employer is legally protected by way of the collecting agency's confirmation.
- The German employer has a paper verifying that the appropriate social security contributions are to be collected in Germany.
- The verification serves as proof for social security audits that the German employer carries out.
- The confirmation of the expatriation applies for all types of German social security.

21 The confirmation further serves as proof that there are no social security contribution obligations abroad. Being double insured is not impossible, however.

What questions arise if the requirements for an expatriation have not been are satisfied?

22 If the requirements for an expatriation have not been satisfied, the application of German social security regulations end when the work abroad begins. Therefore,

there is no longer obligation for the German employer to pay the requisite social security contributions in Germany. A further continuance in German social security (statutory retirement, unemployment, health, long-term care and accident insurances) is, as a rule, possible on a voluntary basis.

Part 4
Income Tax

I. Introduction to the German income tax system

In Germany, income tax is levied on the seven following income types: 1

- Agriculture and Forestry;
- Commercial/Business income;
- Self-employment work;
- Traditional employment;
- Investments;
- Leases and rentals;
- Other income (e.g. pension income).

The amount of income tax will regularly be set through an income assessment notice (Einkommensteuerbescheid) from the German tax authorities (Finanzamt) after the taxpayer (Steuerpflichtige/r) files his or her income tax return (Einkommensteuererklärung). As a rule, income derived by a taxpayer from either investments or traditional employment, income tax is held as a flat tax on investment income (Abgeltungsteuer) by the bank, or by the employer as a payroll tax (Lohnsteuer), respectively, and transferred to the German tax authorities. 2

Except for the taxation of investment income, there is a progressive income tax in Germany ranging from 0–42%. The top tax rate of 45% applies to taxpayers earning 254,447 EUR per annum with an individual tax assessment (Einzelveranlagung), 508,894 EUR for joint filers. Annual income of 8,653 EUR (FY 2016) is tax-free. There are additional taxes beyond income taxes are also collected. They include the so-called "solidarity surcharge" (Solidaritätszuschlag[38]) and the church tax (Kirchensteuer). 3

The solidarity surcharge levies amounts to 5.5% of the income tax. Church taxes are not levied upon all taxpayers who are a member of a religious community, such as the Roman Catholic Church, Old Catholic church, Reformed church, Lutheran church, Unified church, or the Jewish community. That tax varies between 8 and 9%, depending on the federal state (Bundesland) in which the taxpayer resides. 4

As a rule investment income is taxed at 25%, plus solidarity surcharge and, when applicable, church tax. Expenses, as a rule, may not be deducted to reduce one's investment income tax burden. 5

A natural-born person is subject to either limited taxation or is fully taxable (subject to unlimited taxation) in Germany. 6

If a person has a residence (Wohnsitz) or habitual abode (gewöhnlichen Aufenthalt) in Germany, that individual is subject to unlimited taxation on his or her worldwide income. That means that a given taxpayer's foreign-earned income is also fully taxable. Citizenship plays no role in this regard. 7

38 German tax authorities will levy the solidarity surcharge (Solidaritätszuschlag or "Soli") of 5.5% of the actual, individual income tax amount regardless of the taxpayer's nation of origin.

8 A residence is, for example, an apartment or house. It is in this regard crucial that the apartment or house is available for a person to actually reside in. An example of this not being the case might be when the entire building is rented out to a third party. Registration at the local city registry office is not crucial with respect to the occupancy of the residence, however. The actual circumstances are what matters legally.

9 An individual has his habitual abode in Germany if his intention is not to stay in Germany on a merely temporary basis. Exception: the stay in Germany is just for personal reasons (e.g. vacation or hospitalization) and amounts not longer than one year. In particular, a residence will be assumed to be a habitual abode if the individual stays in Germany on a continuous basis for at least six months in that place, though short interruptions are disregarded.

10 An individual without a German residence or habitual abode in Germany is only subject to limited taxation in Germany with his or her income generated from German sources. This would include, for example, rental income from real estate situated in Germany or work physically performed or utilized in Germany.

11 If a person is not only liable for taxes in Germany but also another country, double taxation can take place. In order to avoid this Germany has ratified double-tax treaties (Doppelbesteuerungsabkommen) with most industrialized countries, about 90 in total. However, Germany does not have agreements with them all (i.e. Brazil and Hong Kong). In any event, it is important to know that the regulations of these double-tax treaties take precedence over the German domestic tax laws.

12 If there is no applicable double-tax treaty, Germany can possibly avoid or reduce double taxation through applying a deduction or crediting of foreign taxation toward German taxes based on local German tax law.

13 So long as a person moves either to or away from Germany during a fiscal year, an income tax return must be submitted to the German tax authorities. In that filing, one has to include both taxable German and foreign-earned – even tax-exempt – income. Tax-exempt income is reported for determining a taxpayer's tax rate on Germany's progressive scale. The tax and calendar years are the same in Germany.

14 It is also worth noting that the occupancy of a residence or habitually residing in Germany is relevant to the authorities with respect to inheritance or gift tax liabilities.

15 In general, a German tax resident must file an annual tax return with their local tax office by May 31st of the year following the tax year. This deadline is extended through December 31st of the following year if the return is prepared by a professional tax adviser.[39] Non-residents must file a tax return only under certain circumstances.

39 A further extension may be available upon special request.

The income tax is not payable at the time the tax return is filed. The tax authorities will review the tax return and issue a separate assessment notice (this may take two to six months depending on the tax authorities). Usually, any payment becomes due within one month after receipt of the assessment notice unless separate instructions for payment have been received from the tax authorities. Penalties for late payment are 1% per month of the amount due. 16

Interest is charged or credited on final tax payments if the assessment notice is not issued within 15 months after the end of the tax year. For each month after 15 months following the end of the tax year, 0.5% interest will be charged or credited. 17

II. Inbound

1 **When company assigns an employee to work in Germany, income taxes are an important consideration, and this section is dedicated to presenting some typical questions those assigned to work in Germany have on this matter. Issues such as tax brackets, level of income tax liability, deductions, and what are considered extraordinary expenses in the eyes of German tax laws, among others are addressed here.**

2 **One of those other issues, one that readers may find surprising, is that Germany does collect church taxes for some religions and denominations. This is of significance not only to those countries where church taxes are no longer or have never been collected. The fact that and under what circumstances church taxes are collected in Germany is also important to those residing in countries where church taxes are still collected, like Denmark and Finland, because of the possibility of double taxation.**

3 An employee will be sent on foreign assignment to Germany by his or her employer. Will he or she be subject to German income tax?

4 Regardless of the employee's particular situation, he or she will be subject to either limited or unlimited income tax liability if that employee works in Germany.[40]

5 However, if the employee has **retained his or her residency** in a country with which Germany has a double-tax treaty during his or her time assigned to work in Germany, the limiting provisions of a double-tax agreement between that country and Germany apply.

6 Additionally, keep in mind that the employee on foreign assignment should provide an application for the issuance of a certification for payroll tax withholding for employees with limited tax liability[41] if:

- German tax authorities consider the employee as being subject to limited tax liability;
- the employee's pay is subject to wage tax withholding.

7 This means that the employee's wages will be calculated and withheld in accordance with the lower, "Steuerklasse I" bracket. Otherwise, the withholding from the employee's pay stub will reflect the higher, "Steuerklasse VI" bracket. Generally, "Steuerklasse VI" bracket does not recognize statutory tax exemptions in payroll deduction plans, which ultimately leads to an increased tax burden.

40 See the introduction of the "Income Tax" section for more details about limited and unlimited tax liability.

41 In German form is called "Antrag auf Erteilung einer Bescheinigung für den Lohnsteuerabzug für beschränkt Steuerpflichtige Arbeitnehmer." For a copy of the actual form [German only], visit: https://www.formulare-bfinv.de/ffw/form/display.do?%24context=F141F2C8FA087AB3A7AE.

Wage tax withholdings are regarded to be final for non-tax residents, so the employee does not need to file an annual income tax return in that case. 8

Conversely, if the employee's income is considered fully taxable in Germany, he or she is required to file a German income tax return and some costs can be written off of taxes in Germany. 9

Which costs can be deducted from taxes in Germany?

Under certain circumstances, income-related expenses (Werbungskosten), such as costs incurred for, among other things: 10

- travel between home and work;
- moving costs;
- business trips;
- maintaining two households;
- training/professional development costs;

can be deducted partially or entirely from the employee's taxes. However, this is only the case if the employee's employer has not already reimbursed the given cost(s) and the cost(s) relate to income being taxable in Germany. Without proof (i.e. non-receipted), German income tax laws provides each taxpayer an allowable lump sum of 1,000 EUR per year for work-related expenses. Higher income-related expenses have to be supported with receipts for German tax authorities to recognize those costs.

Further, German law does consider reduced tax rates in certain circumstances for personal or special expenses, such as, among other things: 11

- social security contributions;
- private retirement contributions;
- childcare costs;
- paid church taxes;
- school costs;
- costs for the employee's own professional development;
- charity donations.

In certain other special cases, "extraordinary expenses," such as higher-than-normal medical costs or living expenses for dependents can be deducted from the employee's taxes. 12

Note: Cleaning, handy- or craftsman, or many other local household-related services for official professional usage are also seen as legally permissible tax deductions in some cases. 13

What is a tax ID number (Steueridentifikationsnummer), and how does one get one in Germany?

14 A German tax ID number, sometimes abbreviated as "IdNr," is and individual, 11-digit number. The tax ID number will be generated for the expat by the German Federal Central Tax Office (Bundeszentralamt für Steuern, or "BZSt") after the employee has registered with the employee's city registry office (Meldebehörde) where he or she resides in Germany (in most cases located in the local town hall).

15 The German tax ID number is good for life, regardless of whether the employee has moved or changed his or her marital status. Once the employee has been registered, the number will be generated and the German Federal Central Tax Office will send the employee's German tax ID number per post to the employee's German address. Because this tax ID number is good for the employee's entire lifetime, the official letter with the employee's German tax ID number should be stored in a safe place.

16 The employee should be sure to inform his or her employer in Germany of the German tax ID number also. This is important for payroll accounting, among other reasons. Should the employee on assignment fail to provide his or her employer his or her German tax ID number, the employee's wage deductions will be calculated in accordance with less favorable German "Steuerklasse VI" bracket.

17 Additionally, keep in mind that if the employee loses his or her German tax ID number, it can be resent to that employee after he or she has completed the following online form: https://www.bzst.de/DE/Steuern_National/Steuerliche_Identifikationsnummer/ID_Eingabeformular/ID_Node.html. As one will see, this form, like most others from German organizations, is in German, so do reach out to a German-speaking colleague for assistance if necessary. Once the German tax authorities have received the employee's completed form, the employee's German tax ID number will be resent to the employee by postal service.

How high is the German income tax rate?

18 Due to Germany's progressive income tax rate, as a rule, an individual's precise income tax rate cannot be determined in advance. However, the employee's income tax rate will be between 14% and 42% on a graduated scale if the employee's post-deduction income is between EUR 8,653 and 53,665[42] per annum after deducting the employee's:

- work-related expenses (Werbungskosten);
- personal/special expenses (Sonderausgaben);

42 Between EUR 17,306 and 107,331/annum for those married filing jointly.

- extraordinary expenses, such as extreme healthcare costs) (außergewöhnliche Belastungen).[43]

Those earning between EUR 53,666 to 254,446/annum[44] will be taxed at 42% after deductions. The German tax code reserves the top income tax rate of 45% exclusively for individuals earning EUR 254,447 or more.[45] Important to keep in mind: the solidarity surcharge and, if called for, church tax, will be added on top of the income tax owed. 19

Are expats subject to church taxes and what is the rate?

The employee is subject to church taxes in Germany if he or she is: 20
- a member of certain religious communities, and
- subject to unlimited tax liability in Germany.

Before registering at the local registration office, the assigned employee should confirm whether or not the employee is a member of the Roman Catholic Church, Old Catholic church, Reformed church, Lutheran church, Unified church, or the Jewish community. As a member of one of these religious communities, the employee is automatically subject to church tax, based on the information provided the local registration office. No statutory church tax has to be paid if there is no religious affiliation. Do be aware that inquiries into church affiliation are possible. 21

Neither one's nation of origin or home-country church taxes levied frees someone from paying church taxes in Germany. The German federal states (Bundesländer) of Bavaria and Baden-Württemberg levy an 8% tax on income tax; the rate is 9% on income tax for the other 14 German states. 22

German tax authorities collect church taxes levied on an employee's employment income as a prepayment on the final church tax amount during the fiscal year via payroll deductions. German tax authorities provide a final amount in the employee's income tax assessment notice at the end of the tax year. 23

Special rules on church taxes apply if only one spouse is a member of one of these two denominations, the couple belongs to different religious communities, or in cases where only one spouse works. 24

43 See the following table for some guidance on 2016 tax rates: https://www.bmf-steuerrechner.de/ekst/.

44 Between EUR 107,332 and 50,893/annum for those married filing jointly.

45 Over EUR 508,894/annum for those married filing jointly.

What is an annual wage tax certificate (Lohnsteuerbescheinigung) under German law?

25 A German wage tax certificate, like the W2 in the United States, is the document upon which one's personal payroll accounting is delineated and that employers supply to all of their employees. Being required to have a wage tax certificate is irrespective of whether the employee is subject to limited or unlimited tax liability in Germany.

26 On the wage tax certificate, one will find the following information:

- year-end taxable wages;
- wage taxes withheld by the employer during that fiscal year (including solidarity surcharge and church taxes);
- social security contributions.

27 The wage tax certificate is a tax document that German taxpayers must keep as proof and for the preparation their tax declaration.

What are the ELStAM?

28 The abbreviation ELStAM can be translated into English as electronic wages tax criteria. With the assistance of ELStAM, employers can investigate the monthly (electronic) pay stub the amount of tax withheld from their gross pay.[46]

29 ELStAM provides, for example, information about a taxpayer's:

- tax bracket;
- amount permitted for the German child tax credit (Kinderfreibetrag);
- whether the employee is obligated to pay church taxes.

30 The employer accesses to the employee's ELStAM via the ELStAM databank. For this to work, employers must know the employee's:

- birthdate;
- German tax ID number;
- employment start date;
- additional employment besides his or her primary employment.

31 As a rule, changes to the ELStAM have to be made by the employee at the German tax office in the residential district in which he or she resides.

46 It is extremely uncommon for German employers to pay employees in cash or check. In fact money transfers are commonplace throughout the EU, and, in many cases, are the sole means of distributing or receiving monies/remuneration.

What is meant by the term Progressionseinkünfte?

Per German law, progression income (Progressionseinkünfte) refers to income subject to the exemption with progressive taxation method. More specifically, it generally refers to non-taxable income earned in Germany that is nevertheless included in the annual income tax return in determining to which tax bracket someone belongs. Within a given fiscal year, this applies to: 32
- foreign-earned income that was earned before or after moving to Germany;
- non-taxable income per double-taxation treaty;
- unemployment pay;
- sick pay;
- maternity leave benefit.

This progression income is tax-free in Germany, but remaining taxable income will be taxed at a higher rate, that rate the employee would have been taxed at had all of the employee's income been taxable. Income subject to the exemption via the progressive taxation method therefore indirectly leads to an increased personal income tax rate despite the tax-exempt status. 33

An employee on foreign assignment in Germany will be considered fully taxable while working in living in Germany and is to receive the previous year's bonus during that period. Is that bonus subject to German taxes?

Due to the unlimited taxation liability, the employee's entire worldwide income is subject to German taxes unless the regulations set forth in a double-tax treaty apply. Normally, the bonus would be tax exempt if Germany and the country the employee formerly worked in have a double-tax treaty in place and he or she earned the bonus during a period in which the employee was not liable for German taxes. This also goes for when the employee is already working and living in Germany at the time the bonus is finally paid. However, the bonus has to be declared in the employee's German income tax return as tax-exempt progression income, which leads to an increased personal income tax rate/bracket. 34

Deviations from this can occur if the applicable double-tax treaty includes special rules, or if there is no double-tax treaty in place between Germany and the other country. 35

Generally, Germany will subject bonuses to German taxes so long as there is no evidence that the bonus is not being taxed in another country. 36

The employee's income in Germany will be considered fully taxable and he or she will exercise stock options during his or her time there. Is the income derived from those options subject to German taxes?

37 Due the unlimited tax liability, the employee is subject to income taxes that include the employee's worldwide, or global, income unless double-tax treaty regulations apply. If the country in which the employee was formerly employed has a double-tax treaty with German, income derived from the exercise of stock options is only subject to German taxes if the employee received taxable income in Germany between the grant date and the vesting date (the so-called vesting period).

38 Example: The employee was subject to German taxes during 1/3 of the vesting period. Accordingly, only 1/3 of the profits derived from the stock options exercised in German are subject to German taxes. The remaining portion of the stock options gain has to be declared in the employee's German income tax return as tax-exempt progression income, and this leads to an increased personal income tax rate.

39 For purposes of comparison, if the employee has been only subject to foreign income taxes in the vesting period, the profits are treated as tax-exempt progression income.

40 However, if taxation on the profits abroad cannot be proven, or it cannot be proven that the employee's home country renounces its right to tax the employee's income, the profit will be subsequently subject to German taxes due to its being fully taxable there.

41 Deviations from this can occur if the applicable dual-tax treaty includes special rules, or if there is no dual-tax treaty in place between Germany and the other country.

Does the employer need to provide a payroll accounting for the employee in Germany and pay his or her income taxes, solidarity surcharge, and, if determined applicable, church taxes to German tax authorities?

42 If the employee's legal employer has its headquarters in Germany, or the employee works for his or her permanent establishment (Betriebsstätte) in Germany, the employee's legal employer has to supply an accounting of payroll in Germany and subject any income taxable in Germany to wage tax withholdings. Here, wage taxes, the solidarity surcharge, and (only if applicable) church taxes will be withheld and forwarded to the German tax authorities.

43 Within the context of employee foreign assignments, the company in Germany is obligated to provide an accounting of the assignees' payroll and deduct the appropriate taxes if that company is the so-called "economically determined employer," the one who actually bears the employee's payroll costs, or would be required to do so according to the "arm's length principle". Generally, this is the situation to be assumed in cases of foreign assignments.

III. Outbound

What happens with income taxes when a company assigns an employee coming from Germany to work in another country? Where does he or she need to pay taxes? To what extent do double-taxation treaties play a role in such situations? 1

One of the several outbound topics that is touched upon in this section is one not necessarily understood by companies and workers but with which many are confronted is the concept of the third-party national, or the "third country." These individuals work for multinational companies operating in a foreign country and are citizens in neither the country of employment nor the parent company's home country. Here is an example: 2

John Schmidt is a German national working in the USA at a large US automobile company. The US company sends him to work in Canada, where the automobile model that Mr. Schmidt is working on is produced. John Schmidt is a third-country national in Canada. 3

Thus, third-country nationals differ from expats, as expatriates are recognized as domestic employees on foreign assignment at the behest of a multinational company or its subsidiary. 4

These and many other, related issues require the attention of employees and employers alike when income tax issues related to foreign work assignments arise. This section should help in beginning to clarify these matters. 5

An employer is sending an employee abroad. Does that employee have to continue to pay German income taxes?

This depends on one's personal tax status in Germany during the time he or she will be working abroad. 6

If the employee's habitual abode or residence continues to be Germany, his or her income earned globally will remain subject to unlimited German liability. If one works in a country with which Germany has concluded a dual-tax treaty, possibly restrictive provisions of the double-tax treaty between Germany and the country in which the employee is working are taken into account, whereby Germany must waive its rights to tax in certain circumstances. 7

So long as the employee is subject to only limited tax liability,[47] he or she, as a rule, no longer has to pay German income taxes if that employee: 8

- receives any private income in Germany (e.g. rental income from a property located in Germany);
- receives any subsequent or lagging salary from the employer.[48]

47 Cf. the first paragraph addressing question 1 in this chapter.

48 Cf. questions 4 and 5 of this chapter.

9 A German income tax return needs to be filed in case the employee received any Germany-sourced income that was not initially subjected to withholding taxes; these taxes are generally deemed to be final for non-residents.

The employee's family will remain in Germany during time the employee is working abroad in a country with which Germany is party to a dual tax treaty. The employee will be with his or her family regularly on weekends. What impact does this have on the employee tax-wise?

10 According to the rules of most double-tax treaties, the employee will be counted as a resident of Germany per the applicable double-tax treaty. In most instances, the consequences of this are that Germany retains the right to tax the salary earned during workdays spent in Germany (including home office work), on business travels to foreign countries beyond the one to which the employee is assigned, third countries, or both.

11 The right to tax salary received for work performed in the country to which the employee is assigned applies in Germany only if further conditions have been met.

12 Furthermore, Germany will continue to claim the right to tax any privately earned income (e.g. investment income).

An employee going on foreign assignment rents his or her house or apartment out while on foreign assignment. While on that assignment, the employee lives with his or her family. Does that employee on foreign assignment have to submit an income tax declaration in Germany?

13 Since the employee neither resides nor has habitual abode in Germany, limited tax liability applies for the employee in Germany. This being the case, the employee has to submit an income tax declaration for limited tax liability, in which the employee includes income earned from his or her house or apartment.

An employee receives a bonus for the previous year's work during an assignment abroad. Is that bonus subject to German taxes?

14 An employee bonus is also subject to German taxes if the previous year's income of the employee on foreign assignment was subject to tax during the given earning period in Germany. This remains the case even when the employee no longer lives or works in Germany at the time of the payout.

15 As is the case for inbound expats, if German tax authorities already see the employee as someone subject to limited tax liability in Germany, it is recommended that his or her German employer files the employee's payroll withholding as "Steuerklasse I," German tax bracket one. Otherwise, the employee's payroll withholding will be classified under "Steuerklasse VI," German tax bracket VI. This

would lead to and increased tax burden, since Steuerklasse VI generally does not allow for any statutory tax exemptions.

An employee exercises stock options during the work assignment abroad. Are those earnings subject to taxes in Germany?

Income generated from the exercising of stock options is subject to taxes in Germany, if the employee has drawn income that is taxable in Germany between the time granted and when the options can first be exercised at the vesting date (the so-called vesting period). 16

For example, the employee was subject to German taxes for $^{2}/_{3}$ of the vesting period, $^{2}/_{3}$ of the earnings from the exercised options will be subject to taxes in Germany. 17

On the other hand, 100% of the earnings generated from the options will be taxable in Germany if the employee had been in Germany for the entire vesting period. 18

This lagging salary is then subject to wage tax withholdings in Germany. If the employee counts as being subject to limited tax liability in Germany with the exercising of stock options, it is advisable that the employee requests to have your payroll deductions set at Steuerklasse I.[49] 19

A German employer continued to pay an employee it expatriated while the latter is on work assignment abroad. What is the effect of the foreign assignment on payroll tax withholding?

If the employee continues to be subject to unlimited tax liability in Germany, his or her entire wages are principally subject to German income tax withholding. If the employee works in a country with which Germany has a double-tax treaty and the income is earned in accordance with the tax laws of that country, an application for exemption for German income tax frequently may or may have to be applied for back in Germany. 20

The application needs to be filed with the local tax office of the company of the assigned employee.[50] 21

If the assigned employee is counted as being subject to limited tax liability during your foreign assignment outside of Germany, payroll taxes are then only to be withheld in exceptional cases (i.e. when the employee's employment income is con- 22

49 Cf. Question 5, para. 2 in this chapter.

50 The name of the form is: "Antrag für unbeschränkt einkommensteuerpflichtige Arbeitnehmer auf Erteilung einer Bescheinigung über die Freistellung des Arbeitslohns vom Steuerabzug auf Grund eines Abkommens zur Vermeidung der Doppelbesteuerung".

sidered German-sourced income and an applicable double-tax treaty assigns to Germany the right to tax).

The employee gives up his or her German residency and regular home in Germany during his or her foreign assignment. Does that employee have to notify the German tax authorities or give up his or her German bank account?

23 If the employee moves from Germany, the employee is required to give notice of your departure immediately to the German city registry office (Einwohnermeldeamt) and the German tax office responsible for the given region.

24 It is also recommend that the employee inform his or her bank in Germany that he or she is moving. This can have the effect on the withholding of German taxes (registered as a non-resident for tax purposes (Steuerausländer) on capital income).

25 With dividends from German companies, Germany regularly retains a proportional right to tax in double-taxation agreements. If the full amount of German flat-rate withholding tax (Abgeltungsteuer) is withheld, a reimbursement for the extra taxes paid can be requested from the German Federal Central Tax Office. However, this is entails a considerable amount of effort.

An employee expatriated from Germany for a work assignment assumes that abroad, as compared to in Germany, more taxes must be paid. Is there a solution to this?

26 In practice, there are two possibilities for offsetting this situation that commonly find application that, in connection with the work abroad, the employer and employee can contractually agree upon:

a. Tax Equalization:

27 With this method, the employer pays the actual resulting foreign taxes and, in some circumstances, the additional tax burden in Germany. A hypothetical tax will be withheld – comparable to his or her payroll taxes incurred prior to the foreign assignment – since the employee is considered in Germany as someone who was not working abroad during his or her foreign assignment.

28 German tax authorities will not collect this hypothetical tax. Instead, the employer will use those monies to pay the foreign tax authorities. Should the tax burden abroad be less, the employer will retain the tax benefit. If the actual tax burden abroad is larger, the employer will be required to cover it.

b. Tax Protection:

29 With this method, the employer pays only the additional tax burden. This amount is determined by comparing the actual taxes due in Germany and in the country of assignment with a hypothetical tax. If the employee actually has to pay less tax, he or she need not refund that amount to the employer.

Useful Links

Residence Permit Act (Aufenthaltsgesetz)
http://www.gesetze-im-internet.de/englisch_aufenthg/index.html

Freedom of Movement Act (Freizügigkeitsgesetz)
http://www.gesetze-im-internet.de/englisch-freiz-gg-eu/

Ordinance on Residence (Aufenthaltsverordnung) – in German only
http://www.gesetze-im-internet.de/aufenthv/

Employment Regulation (Beschäftigungsverordnung) – in German only
BeschV – Verordnung über die Beschäftigung von Ausländerinnen und Ausländern

Employment regulation of the federal employment office (Durchführungsanweisungen Beschäftigungsverordnung) – in German only
https://www.arbeitsagentur.de/web/content/DE/Veroeffentlichungen/Weisungen/Arbeitgeber/Detail/index.htm?dfContentId=EGOV-CONTENT442324

Implementing Regulation on employment of foreigners (Durchführungsanweisungen zur Ausländerbeschäftigung)
Degree equivalency database (ANABIN) – in German only
http://anabin.kmk.org/anabin-datenbank.html

Location overview ZAV (employment office) – in German only
https://www.arbeitsagentur.de/web/content/DE/BuergerinnenUndBuerger/ArbeitundBeruf/ArbeitsJobsuche/ArbeitinDeutschland/Arbeitsmarktzulassung/Detail/index.htm?dfContentId=L6019022DSTBAI531395

Department of Foreign affairs – Visa regulations
http://www.auswaertiges-amt.de/EN/EinreiseUndAufenthalt/Uebersicht_node.html

Federal Office for Migration and Refugees
http://www.bamf.de/EN/Startseite/startseite-node.html

International Placement Services (Zentrale Auslands- und Fachvermittlung – ZAV)
https://www.arbeitsagentur.de/web/content/EN/Detail/index.htm?dfContentId=L6019022DSTBAI609149

List of Apostille countries
https://www.hcch.net/en/instruments/conventions/status-table/?cid=41

Social Security information
http://socialwelfare.library.vcu.edu/social-security/social-security-a-brief-history-of-social-insurance/.

Glossary

Deutsch	English
A	
Abgeltungsteuer	flat-rate withholding tax
Abmelden/Abmeldung	de-register/de-registration (with local/city registration office)
Abschiebung	deportation/arrest
AGB-Gesetz (Gesetz zur Regelung des Rechts der Allgemeinen Geschäftsbedingungen)	German Act Governing Standard Business Conditions
Allgemeinverbindlichkeitserklärung	declaration making the agreement generally binding
ANABIN	German (university) degree equivalency database
Antrag auf Erteilung einer Bescheinigung für den Lohnsteuerabzug für beschränkt Steuerpflichtige Arbeitnehmer	application for the issuance of a certification for payroll tax withholding for employees with limited tax liability
Arbeitslosengeld	unemployment pay
Arbeitsunfällen und	Work-related injuries
Arbeitsvisum	work permit
AsylbLG (Asylbewerberleistungsgesetz)	Asylum Seekers Benefits Act
Aufenthaltskarte	residence permit for dependents of EU/EEA/Swiss Nationals
Aufenthaltserlaubnis	residence permit
Aufenthaltserlaubnis-Schweiz	special residence card for Swiss nationals
AufenthG (Aufenthaltsgesetz)	German Residence Act
Auftragsschreiben/Auftragsbestätigungsschreiben	letter of assignment
AÜG (Arbeitnehmerüberlassungsgesetz)	German Temporary Employment Act
außergewöhnliche Belastungen	extraordinary expenses, such as extreme healthcare costs
Auslandseinsatz	foreign assignment/assignment abroad
Ausländerzentralregister	Central Register of Foreigners
ausländische Einkünfte	foreign-earned income, foreign income
Auslandstätigkeitserlass	decree on employment abroad
Ausnahmevereinbarung	Agreement of exemption
Ausreisepflicht	Obligation to leave
Ausstrahlung	outbound (expatriate) employment status (per German law, German employment law follows employee)
Ausweisung	expulsion
Ausweisungsgrund	grounds for expulsion
B	
Beitragsbemessungsgrenze in der allgemeinen Rentenversicherung	social security contribution ceiling
berufsbedingte Kosten	work-related costs

Deutsch	English
Berufsgenossenschaft	German Institution for Statutory Accident Insurance and Prevention
Berufskrankheiten	Work-related illnesses
Bescheinigung für die anzuwendenden Rechtsvorschriften	certificate of coverage
BeschV (Verordnung über die Beschäftigung von Ausländerinnen und Ausländern)	Ordinance on the Employment of Foreigners
beschränkten Einkommensteuerpflicht	subject to limited taxation
Betriebstättenfinanzamt	(local) tax office responsible for the company
Betriebsvereinbarung	works agreement
Bezirksregierung	district or regional council
Bundesagentur für Arbeit	German federal employment agency
Bundesverwaltungsamt	German Federal Office of Administration
BZSt (Bundeszentralamt für Steuern)	German federal central tax office
D	
Daueraufenthalt EG (sometimes "EU")	unlimited residence permit EU
Dienstreise	business trip
Direktionsrecht	Employer's instruction right
Doppelbesteuerungsabkommen	dual-tax treaties
doppelten Haushaltsführung	maintaining of two households
Drittstaatsangehörige	third-country nationals
E	
Einbehalt	withholding, retention
Einkommensteuerbescheid	income assessment notice
Einkommensteuererklärung	income tax return
Einkommensteuersatz	income tax rate
Einstrahlung	inbound (inpatriate) employment status
Einwohnermeldeamt/Meldebehörde	local/city registry office
ELStAM	electronic wages tax criteria
Elterngeld	parental-leave allowance
Entgeltabrechnung	payroll accounting
Entgeltfortzahlung	continued remuneration
Entsendegesetz	posted workers act
Entsendung	posting
Entsendung von Kurzzeitexperten	short-term secondment
Erdienungszeitraum	period of service, servicing period, vesting period, earning period (*all 3 financial)
ELStAM (elektronische Lohnsteuerabzugsmerkmale)	wage tax items, electronic wages tax card
Evangelisch	belonging to the Lutheran Churches of Germany
F	
Festnahme	arrest
Fiktionsbescheinigung	temporary permit
Finanzamt	tax office, tax authorities

Deutsch	English
Freiheitsstrafe	imprisonment
FreizügG/EU (Gesetz über die allgemeine Freizügigkeit von Unionsbürgern)	Act on the General Freedom of Movement for EU Citizens
Führungskräfte	executives
G	
Gehaltsabrechnung	payroll accounting
Geldstrafe bzw. Bußgeld	Monetary fine
gemeinsamer Veranlagung	married filing jointly
Generalvollmacht	general power of attorney
Geschäftsreise	business trip
Gesetz über die allgemeine Freizügigkeit von Unionsbürgern – Freizügigkeitsgesetz/EU – FreizügG/EU	Act on the General Freedom of Movement for EU Citizens
gesetzliche Krankenkasse	statutory (state) health insurance fund
gewöhnlichen Aufenthalt	habitual residence
Grenzpendler	cross-border commuter
Günstigkeitsprinzip	German "favorability principle," deviation from a collective bargaining agreement for the employee's benefit
H	
Handelsregisterauszug	commercial registry
Hausangestellte von Entsandten	Domestic worker/servant of an expat
I	
IHK (Industrie und Handelskammer)	Chamber of Industry and Commerce
im Ausland Beschäftigte	Expatriate, aka "expat" (context: an already employed person residing in foreign country for purpose of working for a given employer in that foreign country)
K	
Kinderfreibetrag	child tax credit, child allowance
Kindergeld	child allowance
Kirchensteuer	church tax
Konzernprivileg	intra-group exemption
Krankengeld	sick pay
Kurzzeitentsendung	short-term posting/assignment
L	
Landgericht	regional court
Langzeitentsendung	long-term posting/assignment
Leistungen an Hinterbliebene	survivor benefits
Leitende Angestellte	executive managers
Lohnsteuerabzug	payroll deduction(s)
Lohnsteuerbescheinigung	annual wage tax certificate

Deutsch	English
M	
Mangelberufe	understaffed occupations
Mitarbeitereinsatz	employee assignment/posting
Mutterschaftsgeld	maternity pay
N	
Niederlassungserlaubnis	settlement permit, permanent residence permit
O	
Ordnungswidrigkeit	administrative offence
P	
Personalüberlassungsvertrag	secondment agreement
polizeiliches Führungszeugnis	police clearance certificate
Progressionseinkünfte	(refers to) income subject to the exemption with progressive taxation method
Progressionsvorbehalt	saving clause regarding progression of taxes (for preventing double taxation)
Projekteinsatz	project (assignment)
Prokura	proxy
R	
Regierungspräsidium	district or regional council
Reiseverbot	Travel ban
S	
SchwarzArbG (Schwarzarbeitsbekämpfungsgesetz)	Control of Unreported Employment Act
Selbstständige Tätigkeit	self-employed entrepreneurs
SGB (Sozialgesetzbuch)	German Social Security Code
Solidaritätszuschlag	solidarity surcharge (on income tax)
Sonderausgaben	personal/special costs
Sozialversicherung	social security
Sozialversicherungszweige	type of social security (benefits)
Standesamt	civil registry/bureau of vital statistics (USA)
Sterbegeld	death/funeral benefit
Steuerausländer	non-resident for tax purposes
Steueridentifikationsnummer	tax ID number
Steuerklasse	tax bracket
Steuermehrbelastung	additional tax burden
Steuerpflichtige/r	taxpayer
Steuertarif	tax rate
Straftat	criminal offense
T	
Tarifvertrag	collective bargaining agreement

Deutsch	English
U	
Ummelden/Ummeldung	Re-register/re-registration (with local/city registration office)
Umzugskosten	moving costs
unbeschränkt steuerpflichtig	subject to unlimited tax liability, fully taxable
Unterhaltsberechtigte	dependents
V	
Verpflegungsmehraufwand	subsistence allowance
W	
Weisungsrecht	borrower's right to instruct his/her employees
Weiterbildungskosten	training costs
Welteinkommen	worldwide income, global income
Werbungskosten	tax-deductible work-related expenses, advertising costs
wirtschaftlicher Arbeitgeber (der den Arbeitslohn für geleistete Arbeit direkt oder indirekt über Weiterbelastungsverträge trägt)	economic employer
Wohnsitz	residence
Wohnungsgeberbescheinigung	landlord confirmation
Z	
ZAV (Zentrale Auslands- und Fachvermittlung)	International Placement Services
zivilrechtlicher Arbeitgeber	company deemed to be your employer under civil law

www.ingramcontent.com/pod-product-compliance
Lightning Source LLC
Chambersburg PA
CBHW080933240926
51849CB00003BA/446